Black Fatherhood

Black Fatherhood

TRIALS & TRIBULATIONS, TESTIMONY & TRIUMPH

Khalid Akil White

ISBN-13: 9781537305653
ISBN-10: 1537305654
Library of Congress Control Number: 2016907681
BLKMPWR, LLC, Fremont, CA

Father (*NOUN*): A MAN WHO has begotten a child; one related to another in a way suggesting that of father to child; *one of the leading men*

Active (*adjective*): characterized by action rather than by contemplation or speculation

Community (*noun*): a unified body of individuals; a group of people with a common characteristic or interest living together within a larger society

Leader (*noun*): a person who has commanding authority or influence (*Merriam-Webster's Online Dictionary, 2009*)

Fathers are expected and assumed to be the leaders of their family and leaders within their respective homes. When combined, homes and families form our neighborhoods. When put together, our homes, families, and neighborhoods comprise our communities. Together, communities build cities. Cities, when connected together, create states.

Mass media and popular culture bombards us with so many negative, stereotypical portrayals of "the irresponsible Black man." The missing "baby daddy." The "deadbeat dad," the absentee father, the incarcerated Black male, the hyper-masculine Black male, the drug addicted Black male, and so forth. Does art imitate life regarding our Black men?

Seemingly, an endless number of Black men are "absent." They are absent from their families, their homes, and their communities. With so many Black men missing, is there any wonder why Black America appears to be in such disarray? Male leadership is lacking. By and large, the Black man is gone in so many instances for a myriad of reasons.

But wait…there is hope for our beloved Black community! All is not lost!

In the face of such harrowing, negative statistics, stereotypes, and imagery and in light of such negative media portrayal, there *are* scores of Black men who have taken the responsibility of fatherhood head on. We often overlook those men and fathers who *are* present, active, and hands-on in their children's lives. The active, present, accountable Black father—the role model, the leader—also deserves an opportunity to be documented, portrayed, and highlighted. He is not an anomaly! I know firsthand that there are two sides to the Black fatherhood story.

Through this project, my intentions are to reflect on both sides of the story to provide a sense of balance, positivity, and hope for Black fathers and for the Black community as a whole. By offering a more balanced, positive Black male image, it is my hope that the personal stories shared within can help inspire and empower other Black fathers on *their* personal journeys.

This project isn't to suggest that those involved have all the answers or that they are perfect, nor is it meant to belittle anyone in any way. It is a chance to bring light to African American men who are actively involved in their children's lives, those men who have accepted their responsibilities with regards to fatherhood—the trials and tribulations as well as the triumphs.

I knew the men involved offered a unique, personal story to share with the public. There are other brothers, other fathers that are in similar situations. In building and reshaping our community, their personal stories can help inspire, empower, reinforce, and reinvigorate a community of African American men to be the leaders that our next generation deserves and needs.

Thank you.
Khalid Akil White, EdD

Table of Contents

Foreword by Rev. Dr. Larry Wayne Ellis

I looked for someone among them who would build up a wall and stand before me in the gap on behalf of the land so I would not have to destroy it, but I found no one.

EZEKIEL 22:30
NIV

I BEGIN MY JOURNEY BY stating that it was the absence of a father that drove me early on to be present in my children's lives if I ever had any. The desire was born out of two early recollections. In elementary school my single mom never came to school events because of her work schedule. Automatically I felt different and less fortunate than my two-parent peers. Even though they were few in number, they stood out like a bright light. My nonpresent-parent friends and I bonded as a result of this recognition.

Secondly, my mom married a "hustler" after already having six kids by different men. As hustlers do, he beat my mom and used her paycheck to support his lifestyle. I swore if I ever married I would never be like that creep. I remember solidifying this promise to myself at age sixteen.

I had my first serious romance as a college freshman, and my girlfriend became pregnant after about the fourth encounter of unprotected sex. And we had a beautiful daughter. I had worked since I was sixteen and could afford to be married, but she declined my offer. I was devastated because I had made the promise to myself. Nevertheless, as I moved to California after college, I took care of her in all manners. We adored each other.

I married for the first time at twenty-six years of age. The first three years were great, as we had two boys. After I was called into ministry, the end came after a few more years.

My ex-wife believed that I was the more stable parent, so she "gave" me the boys to raise. I was a single dad for nearly three years. Today I have celebrated my twenty-fifth anniversary with my current wife, a wonderful lady. She has helped raise our children.

I kept my promise to myself. I have been there for every event and supported my kids without fail. Two of my now adult children are married with children, and the final one is looking seriously. I believe that what we model every day is the most important teaching tool. Our children need to see love in action. It is more beneficial than all of the toys one may give or receive.

The work of a father and now grandfather is my most important role. I still cherish the moments we share. I make opportunities for time together with them individually and as a group. African American men as myself do take this role of parenting to heart. One of my contributions to Black family life was to be trained as a marriage and family therapist. I have shared countless families' strategies to become more loving and caring people.

I know that this project will transform many lives because of its focus and my desire to make a positive impact. If I have learned anything, it is that at the end of life's journey, what your family says about you, especially what your children and their children say, will mean more than all of the accolades, achievements, and accomplishments from all sources combined. It is my honor to share my thoughts on this important matter.

Use the hyper link for more details:
https://youtu.be/wpBcKAZzzPY

Preface by Dr. Khalid Akil White

*Waitin' for the Lord to rise, I look into my daughter's eyes
and realize I'mma learn through her.
The Messiah might even return through her
If I'mma do it, I gotta change the world through her.*

COMMON, *"BE (INTRO)", 2005*

ADMITTEDLY, I AM A HIP-HOP lover. Hands down, unabashed, no doubt about it. I grew up an '80s baby in love with the lyricism, consciousness, graffiti art, dancing, dress, hairstyles, DJing, and all else that hip-hop culture embodies. I love lyricism. I love the wordplay, similes and metaphors, double entendres, and pictures painted in my mind by skilled wordsmiths. To me, that is hip-hop.

It was in late 2008 that I heard the lyrics quoted above by the artist Common in his song entitled "Be (Intro)." It was and still is a dope song.

I'd listened to the song multiple times. I mean, "Be" came out in 2005. I'd heard it several times through the years. Yet as a hip-hop lover, here I was listening to the song again in 2008.

It's just that in 2008, this song and that line, had so much more meaning to me. Those lyrics had so much more depth related to my personal life. Those words hit home with thunderous impact. Those specific, particular lines, those four bars, gave me the chills that day. They made me get emotional.

The way Common expressed it, that was *exactly* how I felt about my own daughter, Khaliah. To me, hearing those bars was like hearing an angel speaking in my ear. Those lyrics took me to another place.

Hearing those lines from Common prompted me to want to express my personal story regarding my daughter. I consider myself as being a proud father. From this idea, I felt it was incumbent upon me to help give voice to other Black fathers in sharing pieces of their own stories of fatherhood.

So in the esteemed words of one of the greatest hip-hop lyricists, style innovators, and a father himself, Biggie Smalls, "Listen up. I got a story to tell."

Khalid White
"I Got a Story to Tell"

IT WAS JUNE 2006. I was twenty-five years old, going on twenty-six that fall. I'd recently moved back home to the Bay Area from being out of state for college. I had earned my bachelor's and master's degrees at Morehouse College and Harvard University School of Education, respectively. Plus, I'd just landed one of those "good jobs" paying over $25 an hour, full time, with benefits and overtime available. *You couldn't tell me I wasn't the man.*

In my mind, I was blessed. I was young, worry-free, handsome, educated and I thought I was smooth. To top it off, I was about to make some "real money" now. I was getting ready to execute my five-year plan. The plan included financial freedom, traveling, beautiful women, and a rapid ascent up the socioeconomic ladder.

You see, I was positioning myself to embark upon the lifestyle of a true player, inclusive of all the trappings that lifestyle offers. A player's life is celebrated in hip-hop culture, the culture of my peers and I. Naturally I couldn't wait to begin my own celebration.

Many of my homies, some homegirls and my hip-hop idols touted that player lifestyle. And I felt like my time had arrived to enter into that echelon: the coveted player's circle. I had *every intention* of becoming Player of the Year in 2006.

I was on top of the world. Money wasn't going to be an issue. I was about to start getting paid. I was actively dating. I definitely wasn't trying to be attached to *any one* woman. I had a decent little ride, my own spot. Life was good…and it was improving daily.

Some of my friends already had kids of their own. And, although I love kids, having a child of my own was definitely not in my immediate-future plan. Whenever the question was posed to me, "Do you have any kids?" my answer was an emphatic "Hell nah." Having kids would definitely derail my player aspirations. In fact, kids would derail just about every plan I'd conjured up for myself over the next five years.

A few months passed and in late August 2006, I received a phone call that stopped me dead in my tracks. The call was from a young lady I had been seeing. Yes, we were seeing each other. But I let it be known that I wasn't interested in anything long term. I didn't see myself settling down or being attached to any woman at that point in my life.

During that phone call, she went on to articulate that she was pregnant…
with *my* child.

Wait. *What?*

Admittedly, I was devastated. I was floored. How could *this* happen? Why? I
wasn't ready to be a dad. I wasn't ready to commit to any woman long term.
I was beyond *pissed!*

Receiving that news, I felt like I let my family down. How could I tell them
this news? Ultimately, I'd really let myself down. I felt like this was the end of
the world for me. I used to pride myself on *not having* kids. Being able to give
that "hell nah" answer about having kids was golden to me. Now look at me.
Just as I was about to become that man I'd always envisioned I'd become. Shit!

On TV or in the movies, I'd seen so many times where men and women
would be overjoyed when they got the news of a pregnancy. They'd jump for
joy. They'd tell their friends how excited they were. They'd say gleeful, yet
corny, phrases like, "OMG. Babe, guess what…? We're pregnant!"

For me, getting this news was nothing short of a death sentence. It was
scary. No joy involved whatsoever. I now felt overwhelmed, stressed, crushed.
I was depressed. Life as I knew it was coming to a crashing end.

I wished it was all just a bad dream. Yup, I'd wake up, dust myself off, and
keep it moving—child-free, of course.

Needless to say, it wasn't a dream. It was my new reality. I was not happy
with the news at all. I felt stranded. Alone. Here I was, in a situation I didn't
want to be in. In a situation I wasn't equipped to handle. And involved with a
woman I didn't envision myself with long term. I felt down and out. Scared.
Angry. All at once. What was I going to do?

I am ashamed to admit it now, but I contemplated packing up, changing
my phone number, leaving that "good job," and heading out solo to Atlanta.
Maybe there no one would find me. Out there I could live child-free. I'd do
my thing as a single man with no kids. In Atlanta, I'd be out of sight, out of

mind. No child to take care of. No woman to be bothered with, and a fresh lease on life. Yes, that would be perfect. Atlanta was my answer! It was where all my worries would cease.

I could understand it now. I could really understand how guys could just walk out on their child's mother and leave the kid. I mean, that's what I felt like doing. Leaving would solve all my problems. In this case, leaving was my best move. I'd just cut myself completely out of the equation. I had it all figured out.

As I planned my clever "escape" to Atlanta, it hit me. I recalled all the men in my life. My own dad. My sports coaches. My grandfathers. Mentors. My Uncles. My Pastor. All of these male role models I'd had in life. I wondered how they felt when they got the news they'd be dads. Did they feel happy? Did they want to run, want to escape? Did they feel like I was feeling? Or was I tripping? Maybe I was just overreacting. Like Slick Rick said, "This type of shit happens every day," right?

I had an epiphany reflecting over these men. Through the years, they took time, effort, and energy to mold and guide me into the young man I was. What if they had walked away? Where would I be? How would I have ended up? Life would've been so much different for me if I hadn't had them.

I reflected on my own father and our relationship. To this day, he's still a huge presence in my life. He could've gone his own way when he and my mother's relationship didn't work out. But he didn't, thankfully. He stayed an active, present figure in my life, despite the personal circumstances he faced.

I remember as a kid being raised with my uncles, John and Earl. I recall them teaching me things like how to catch a baseball, wrestling moves, how to hop a fence, and how to barbeque. Life's lessons. On top of that, my uncles remained there for their own sons and families.

I could see both of my grandfathers. I remember they used to cook for and take care of my brother and I as kids. Right or wrong, they stayed down and raised their kids.

I reflected on my spiritual father, Pastor Ellis. He was even a single dad for a while. I knew he'd be disappointed in me if I left my child out there alone, fatherless.

I thought about some of my homies. They were doing their best to be active fathers for their kids. Whether they were raised with their own dads or not, they remained proud, active fathers in their kids' lives.

A few of the homies told me to chill out. I was in a good position. They were happy for me as an expecting dad. They ensured me that having my own child wouldn't be the end of the world like I saw it. In fact, it would be a new beginning.

I knew the women in my family would look down on me too if I up and left. They'd think less of me for leaving another Black woman to raise *my child* all by herself.

All in all, I wouldn't be able to look at myself in the mirror if I left a child of mine helpless. I'd be too ashamed. Handling responsibilities is paramount in my life.

No matter how bad I wanted to, no matter how I rationalized and justified leaving my unborn child, I couldn't do it. I couldn't abandon my child and live with a clear conscience. The type of person I am, that would have eaten me alive.

I was blessed to have my dad, uncles, and both maternal and paternal grandfathers in my own life, not to mention, my mother, aunts, and grandmothers. How could I run away from one of the biggest responsibilities life was presenting me? They hadn't.

It took me a long while to come to grips with the fact that I'd soon be a dad. As the time neared for my daughter Khaliah to be born, I had to accept it. I felt I was at a crossroads in life. I had to man up, accept my responsibility, and be a father to my child. But I didn't really know how to do it. All the how-to books in the world couldn't help me. But *I had to do it*. I had to stay. I had to be there for her. I prayed for help.

May 11, 2007, changed my life forever. I'll never forget that night. I watched my We-Believe-era Golden State Warriors beat the Utah Jazz in the playoffs that night in the delivery room. That was the famous game where Baron Davis dunked on Andrei Kirilenko.

My daughter Khaliah was born that same evening. And honestly, *nothing* has been the same since. Quite frankly, life has improved for me on the whole, following her birth.

Khaliah's birth also brought my family closer over time. Her birth brought so much more focus to my life. Becoming a father has helped me to mature, become less selfish, and look toward the future, toward a bigger picture. My life is still a work in progress. But fatherhood has enhanced all facets.

Having a daughter has made me view myself and my relationships with women in a completely new way, with a whole new lens. That player lifestyle was never really me. It was never really for me. My mental state then was so damaged. In turn, it damaged a lot of my interactions with women in the past. I can't blame hip-hop culture, TV, my friends, or anyone else for my decision-making. I was just young and dumb. I was just trying to find who I really was.

Fast forward to the current year. I can't begin to imagine myself without my daughter. My life before fatherhood was so shallow, so shortsighted.

Being a father is a role that not everyone is given, nor can everyone embrace it. It is such a blessing to have a child. But it's definitely not an easy task. The role is not a glamorous one. There isn't much instant gratification in this line of work. Nine times out of ten, things definitely don't change or improve over-night. Nor does the task come with instructions or a how-to booklet. There's no app that you can download to learn how to be a daddy.

However, in terms of sheer impact, in terms of indescribable joy, the role is incomparable. In terms of absolute necessity, the role of a father is essential. The role of fathers is *particularly essential* in the Black community. The role of fathers as active leaders is mandatory for our collective survival.

So like Common's lyrics suggest, I now realize "I'mma learn through her...if I'mma do it, I gotta change the world through her."

Nowadays, when asked if I have kids or if I am a dad, my reply is an emphatic and proud "Absolutely." Sometimes, it's even an emphatic "Hell yeah."

William Cherry
"Fatherhood Near and Far: Reflections from a Long-Distance Dad"

Although black fathers are more likely to live separately from their children...many of them remain just as involved in their kids' lives...67 percent of black dads who don't live with their kids see them at least once a month...there's compelling evidence that the number of black dads living apart from their kids stems from structural systems of inequality and poverty, not the unfounded assumption that African-American men somehow place less value on parenting.

Statistics by Pew Research Center
From the article
"The Myth of the Absent Black Father"
by Tara Culp-Ressler
www.thinkprogress.org
January 16, 2014

I believe a good father must be a God-fearing man, a role model...take on responsibilities and be willing to make sacrifices to ensure his child or children's needs are met.

WILLIAM CHERRY

I FIRST MET WILLIAM "WILL" Cherry, a long-distance dad, about eight years ago. He and I were both employed by the same city-government agency. In fact, he had been working in the department for five years prior to my arrival on the job. He helped train me, took me under his wing, and showed me the ropes on the job. We hit it off pretty well and remained cool even after I'd moved on professionally.

During time spent shooting the breeze on the job, I saw he and I shared some commonalities. Will noted that he too went to a HBCU (Historically Black College and University) in the South. He too was a fan of the San Francisco 49ers. And he too had daughters. As we got to know each other more, he further opened up. Will opined about how having girls had changed his outlook on life as a man.

From our conversations at work, I knew Will had a unique perspective on being a Black father. Will's perspective on fatherhood was one that I could definitely learn something from. For one, he was ten years older than me. He had more time in the "daddy game" than me. Secondly, his daughters were older than mine. He shared some advice on enjoying the time that they are young, cute, and cuddly. As he put it, "It ain't gonna stay that way forever." In short, I figured he had more experience in parenting than I did. He must know a little something, right?

Lastly, and perhaps most strikingly, Will was successfully balancing parenting daughters that he and his wife had in California. Meanwhile, he was also parenting a daughter that *lived in the state of Florida* with her mother.

Wait. What? That last fact caught me completely by surprise. I was unaware of that. I thought, "How do you pull that off? How does that work?

Does your wife know about the daughter in Florida? You have to explain that one to me, bro."

The more I thought about it, the more I realized I knew a couple of brothers who had kids who lived out of state, or at least way out of the area. I thought about how challenging that scenario must be on multiple levels for everyone involved: father, mother, and kids.

Whether it is having their children during school breaks, using technology to Face Time and Skype regularly, or taking road trips to see their kids, these brothers seemed to be making it work as "long-distance dads." Despite the circumstances they faced in distance apart, these men remained as active and as present as they could be. Men like William don't let distance dictate their desire and determination to be a dedicated dad.

I wanted to find out about Will's father and their relationship. Will added that "my relationship with my father is great. I still seek his advice. I believe my parenting style is like my father's."

Will went on to say that his "father was the ideal father figure. I knew growing up that my father wasn't one of my friends. If I did something I shouldn't have, my father had no problem reminding me he was the parent."

He added that his dad, William Cherry, Sr. "stressed education, morals and goals, watched his actions and how he carried himself around me. He understood that later in life I'd strive to be like him."

According to Will, "My relationship with my father impacted my development as a man. My father taught me to accept challenges, to not be afraid to make mistakes, to strive to be the best man you can be."

"My father didn't have the opportunity to spend a lot of time, but when he did I valued that time. I really strive not to allow this to happen to my children as much as I can."

This includes Will physically spending time with his daughter who resides in Florida.

Naturally curious, I wanted to delve deeper into Will's decision-making process around this scenario. How did he arrive at his choice to leave Florida and relocate to California? How was it determined that his daughter would not relocate with him? How did he maintain that long-distance relationship? How did Will keep up his presence and activity with his daughter and, subsequently, with her mother?

WILL: The decision to move to another state without my oldest child, Tanya, was *very* difficult. But I felt like I had to do it. I shared with my daughter's mother, my friends, and my own father of how much this decision was weighing on me and starting to give me second thoughts. I was torn.

My daughter Tanya was seven years old at the time. In the second grade. I really wrestled with the questions of could I be a long-distance parent *and* still be effective? Would my child's relationship with me be *damaged forever*?

Living apart from Tanya, in another state, is difficult. As you could imagine, the distance between us just makes it *tough*. I can't be there to provide a hug when she has a bad day. I can't physically make every parent/teacher meeting. You know, those type of things may *seem* little on the surface but they are *real important to me*. It really takes a lot of sacrifice on everybody's part.

But I talk to my daughter several times a week. I have lived out of state for several years now, so she has adapted and adjusted to it with time. She calls me often when she has questions, and we communicate regularly. She and I also visit very often. And that makes things a lot easier for both of us.

My role is to be there financially and emotionally and to be a positive role model to her. A lot of the time that means I am the one that has to say no. But I'm not here to be her friend and, hopefully, Tanya understands that.

Tanya is now fifteen years old. Will's younger daughters, Denise and Dana, are now nine and six years old, respectively.

Will provided his advice to other Black fathers parenting in similar circumstances to those he's dealing with.

WILL: If the relationship between you two is over or it's not going anywhere, both parents gotta find common ground and make sure you stay there. So when it was finally decided that we'd no longer be together, then co-parenting became our top priority. We both agreed and understood that Tanya needed to have both parents active in her life regardless of the relationship ending.

I only ask that we never put each other down in front of our daughter. As parents, sometimes we do disagree. Disagreements will come. But don't put the child in the middle of it to be a referee. Just meet the child's needs as best you can. Now, again, it took a lot of time, effort, and energy for us to even get it to this point.

Will also took a little time out to expound on the importance of communication and co-parenting with Tanya's mother.

WILL: I've been lucky because Tanya's mother has been very supportive. She's kept me in the loop as Tanya's father. She works well with communicating with me to ensure that Tanya feels supported. So together *we* decide what is best for our child. The distance makes it challenging, but we both do a great job of being active in Tanya's life. *Our* best efforts make a lot of difference.

WILL: Men, *please do not allow the distance to stop you from being a father.* Stay active. Communicate often because communication is the key, especially long distance. Attempt to be open minded with the other parent's suggestions. Attempt to come to a middle ground with her if you can.

Brothers, just remember that if we don't take the roles of a teacher and a role model for our children, their peers, the streets, or the society will. The first male a child encounters is their father. So you have a great opportunity to set the tone of what a male is. I believe the more active our fathers are, the Black community will grow and prosper. It could help bond the African American community as a whole.

Being a father is a calling that comes with lots of responsibility. It comes with making choices and sacrifices. But the reward of watching your child grow, the reward of being your child's "superhero," your child's favorite man in the world. It's really a priceless feeling.

Marlin Brown
"Faith, Family, and Football"

*A young man without a male role model
is like an explorer without a map.*

The Steve Harvey Morning Show

*'Cause if it wasn't for those tests and me goin' through some
adversity and some challenges, I wouldn't be the man I am
today. If life was easy, everybody would have a big house
with ten bedrooms and an elevator. Life's not easy.*

MARLIN BROWN

Marlin Brown is the kind of man whose presence is felt immediately. He's the kind of man who is hard to forget. As soon as he enters the room, you'll know who Marlin Brown is. At times a very comical and entertaining guy, he is also a very outspoken extrovert.

Standing 6'3 and weighing 275 pounds. Marlin strikes an imposing figure. He was a former terror to opposing quarterbacks on the gridiron. And he brings the same passion and zeal that he once had for playing football into all areas of his life.

A memorable personality indeed, Marlin offers an interesting perspective on life's three F's: faith, family, and football. He even provides insight on growing up biracial and raising biracial children.

Marlin is blessed with an adoring and growing family. And it was obvious to me that his huge presence was even larger when he was in the comfort of his own home. His sons hung onto him physically. And they also hung on his every word.

The outspoken Brown was not shy in sharing with me about his family.

MARLIN: [I've been] happily married to my beautiful wife for the last thirteen years. Her name is Joy Brown. My beautiful daughter, Jasmine Marie Brown, she's twenty-three years old. My beautiful, first-born son, Marlin Ben Brown, he's eleven years old. My handsome son, Jamar Darien Brown, he's nine years old. And the one and only M.J., Marcus Jovan Brown, he's six years old. And I have a wonderful grandson. Andrew James Valley. He's three years old.

I'm a lead group supervisor at the Youth Services Center Juvenile Hall, for the last sixteen years. These kids are incarcerated. Locked down. So my job as a lead group supervisor is to supervise the youth. Take care of their safety, security, control of their meals, their education programs, make sure they have all the resources that they need. Everything. From essays, artwork, poetry, to large-muscle activity. I truly enjoy it. I haven't saved all the kids I've worked with, but I've definitely touched their lives. I work with boys and girls. Currently, I'm with the young ladies. And that's goin' really well.

We started the Becoming a Man program in the hall to help the young men. It's an evidence-based program, meaning it's been done before, and it's actually shown to reduce juvenile recidivism. It's a program I did strictly for the young boys. It's taught them everything from responsibility to accountability to overcoming adversity to persevering.

Each staff member—Black, White, male, or female—gives their expectations of what a man is. Then we would give the youth an opportunity to speak. Thirty boys in a circle. We'd propose a question, and they would answer the question. We'd go around. There were some very magical moments in that program. Moments where both youth and staff were cryin' and just lettin' it out.

Ones that I've worked with and counseled over the sixteen years, they're very angry with their father. He's either not around, he left. He hit the mom. He wasn't a very good role model. However, it's back to this point. There's only two type of people: those that *bless you* and those that *test you*. These kids were sent a negative individual who tested 'em. They can learn from that test. Or they can repeat it. So a lot of these young men are very angry with their fathers, and they've discussed it in the program with me, at length.

I've tried to teach them that at some point you gotta forgive your father. Once you forgive, then you begin to heal. All I can do as a group supervisor is instill the good qualities of men. Show them what a man's supposed to do: responsibility, accountability, perseverance, and respect. I have to lead by example. And I make sure I'm doing those things when I'm with them.

All I can do is give them some tools to put in their toolbox. Whether they pull it out and use it is totally up to them. For the young ladies I work with, I have to show them this is what a real man does, how he treats females.

All of these kids want somebody to listen to them. Better yet, they want somebody to *hear* them. And if you listen to them, you know, ask a key question, and then just be quiet, they will give you everything they have. And by listening to them, you can find out how to make them wealthy. And by wealthy I mean mentally, physically, financially, and emotionally wealthy. If I feed them some positive information on how to handle anger, how to handle grief, sadness, death, then they'll get a little bit healthier emotionally.

My advice to anybody that's gonna be workin' with these kids is to listen. It's a wonderful field to get in. You get a lotta self-enjoyment, self-fulfillment from doing it, and it's decent money. Try to help them. Point them in the right direction. Have some pertinent information ready for them. Introduce them to the right people that can help them on their journey. And, if that right person is you, so be it.

I don't know about the "ideal man," but the man that I have become and that I am teaching my sons and my grandson to become is somebody that's all about God. Somebody that's all about family, all about havin' their families' back, being a good person and blessing others.

When you bless others, it comes back to you automatic. I'm a big believer in that. If you want to be evil and wicked toward people, that will come back on you too. So I'm just teaching my kids to be inspirational as well as be inspired. Be strong as well as share your strength and to always put God first. God and family, that's what we're about.

I had a football coach at a very young age named Jack Allen. Jack Allen was the best. Tongans, Samoans, African Americans, Latinos, Caucasian, Asians, Filipinos, everybody saw Coach Allen, who was an African American man, as a coach, as a dad, as a mentor. He cared about all of us. I emulated Jack Allen. And Brent Williams, a Caucasian head football coach of mine at Aragon High School. Men of different races have had a big influence on my life. My own father, Benjamin Franklin Brown, Jr. was a great man. God rest his soul. He passed away a few years ago, but all of these men helped me to be a good man.

And on the flipside of that, my beautiful mother also instilled in me how to be a good man from a woman's point of view. My mother was more of the "I love you. I'm proud of you. You can do it no matter what" type of lady. And my father was more of the "You're *gonna* do this and get it accomplished *right now.*" And I understood both very well.

[My father and I] had a strong relationship. I didn't live with him, but he always was in contact with me. I'm very passionate, and I'm very outspoken. I speak my mind, and that's all due to my father. I'm comfortable in front of a crowd, in front of a group, in front of anyone. I can have a conversation with anybody, from any walk of life. I get that all from my father. Also like me, he loved God and family. He taught me a whole lot in those areas.

My father taught me a lot of good things, a lot of good qualities. Speaking up for yourself. Stand up straight. Always looks a man in his eye. Always be respectful. Never be disrespected.

He was a very strong man, a musician. He loved music. He played the piano, the flute, the drums, and he played the bass guitar. He was a master musician. He played a little bit of reggae, a little bit of rhythm and blues. Just an outstanding performer. He did it all. He had a group called Macaw.

So when he passed away, I made sure that I listened to his music all the time. I still listen to it to this day. And he still lives on through his music. My nine-year-old son Jamar actually looks a lot like him. All my aunties and uncles will say, "Jamar, he looks just like Ben."

My dad was the first of ten children. I'm the first of over two hundred grandchildren. Being the first grandchild, I've given the family four more additions, my beautiful daughter and three sons. The Brown name lives on and on.

I'm not a perfect man by any means. My kids have heard me cuss. My kids have seen me lose my cool. But they've also seen me apologize and say, "Daddy shouldn't have did that. That was wrong." I'm tryin' to show my sons how to be a good man. When you do wrong, make sure you atone for it with an apology *and* with corrective actions. Learn from that, and never make the same mistake.

You have to instill things in them at an early age. Whether you know it or not, as a parent, the way you act, the way you treat others, the things you say. Your kids are watching your every move.

So from the time I was born, at least as long as I could remember, everybody told me, "You're gonna play football. You're gonna get a scholarship. You're gonna be good, man." That's all I was told. So that's what I did. The sport of football is a team sport. One of the main things it's teaching is teamwork.

With the sport of football, you have to be very aggressive. You have to be very assertive. You have to be moving at all times. You have to be willing to hit another individual. But what I'm teachin' my sons about the sport is that it can take you from a game as a child, to an experience as a teenager, to a scholarship and getting your entire college paid for, to even a professional career. But what they're learning right now is how to be cohesive with a team of different people, different individuals.

We're teachin' how to overcome adversity. You're gonna face adversity on every football team. Injuries, bad calls, bad decisions. You have to learn to overcome all of these things. You have to work as a team. We learn to be decent with each other. We learn to atone for what wrong you've done or said. So football, with the right coaches, can be one of the most wonderful life experiences in the world.

But if you learn from some good coaches, good men, good fathers and mentors, learn the proper techniques, learn teamwork, discipline, controlled aggression, usin' your strengths at the right time, all of these things become life lessons on and off the field. Before every game I would pray. And after every game I said a prayer. So faith, family, and football is what I've always been about and I'm transferring that over to my sons. They're listenin'. And doin' a very good job.

There's only two types of people in this world: those who will bless you and those who will test you. If it wasn't for those tests and me goin' through some adversity and some challenges, I wouldn't be the man that I am today. If life was easy, everybody would have a big house with ten bedrooms and an elevator. Life's not easy. You're gonna get knocked down, and you're gonna have haters.

You're gonna run into racism. You're gonna run into skepticism, tests. If you start running from everything that's hard, you're gonna be doing a lot of runnin'. I've seen racism because of who I am. But I've seen more love, more people who didn't care what color I was. They just liked me for who I was. And it had nothin' to do with race.

My beautiful mother is an Italian American. My father is an African American. God rest his soul. I have a beautiful wife who happens to be Filipino. We have a little joke that our children can go Mike Tyson, Rocky Marciano, or Manny Pacquiao. So you really don't wanna mess with us!

My mother and father, my family, they're like, "You're Marlin Brown. You're a Brown. We're proud of you, and we love you." And that's all I'm tellin' my kids. I have been teased for bein' multiracial. Called names like Zebra, Oreo, etc. But it only made me stronger. I know who I am.

You are who you are. You're born to who you're born. Your mother and father are your mother and father. So that's what I'm tryin' to teach my kids. There's no racism in our family. All I'm teaching them is to love and protect yourself from those who wanna do you harm.

I can't teach my kids to be Black or Filipino or Italian. I'm not gonna teach 'em to "act Black," to "act White." I'm not gonna teach 'em to "act Filipino." I'm gonna teach 'em to be Browns. They are half their mother and half their father. So however my kids are actin', they learned that from my wife and I. I can just teach them to be proud of themselves. But we are very proud members of the African American race, the Italian race, the Filipino race, and moreover, the human race.

My boys have a White grandmother, a Black grandmother, and a Filipino grandmother. They don't see Black grandma. They don't see Filipino grandma. They don't see Italian grandma. They see Grandma. They see Grandma Rosetta. And that's Mama Josie. It took a while for each of one of these kids to figure out that they were multiracial. A father teaches his sons and daughters to be the best they can be. But race is a part of that. Don't get me wrong.

You'll never hear me say the N-word. You'll never hear that come out of my sons' mouths. That's just something I'm teaching them. Just teaching 'em to be good young men.

And my daughter, she's also multiracial. Her mother is half African American, half Italian, as I am. But you know, I'm so proud of that young lady. She is bein' a great mother, a great role model to the youth that she's workin' with. And that's due to her hard work and God. She's grown. Got her own place, got her own car, has a wonderful job, and she's doin' marvelous things.

So I'm startin' that same process with my boys so they see me be a good father. They're seeing me be a good husband, very faithful to my wife. That's my queen, my heart. That's all they hear. Respect, love, strength, and focus.

My wife, she's all of that. I love this woman with all my heart. From the moment she came into my life, my life changed for the better.

When I met her, something just told me, "Go ahead and share with her that I have a daughter." And I met her at the club…love at the club, which usually never works out.

I said to her, "By the way, I have a beautiful daughter. She's four years old." Her answer was what captivated me. Her answer was, "I can't wait to meet her." From the moment she met my daughter, they hit it right off. We just instantly fell in love. That was in 1996. She helped me raise my beautiful daughter. She gave me three beautiful sons.

She's just been a great, great blessing to me as my wife, my queen, as the mother of my children, as my best friend, as my mentor. I'm eight years older than her, but I've learned so much from this beautiful woman. Without her, this wouldn't work. I wouldn't be the strong man that I am. I wouldn't be as confident as I am. My sons wouldn't be as confident and happy as they are. When you hear people say, "I'm happily married," some of 'em are woofin'. I can say that with confidence. "I'm happily married with children."

So my advice to brothers out there is be very cautious and be very careful of the woman you pick. Don't ask someone to marry you unless you are serious. Marriage is for real. Fatherhood is for real. There are good people out there. But it's up to you to find 'em. I found mine. And I'm gonna keep her.

Douglas Fort
"Becoming a Whole Person for Team Fort"

*With its "War on Drugs" era and mandatory sentencing
procedures, black men have been unfairly targeted,
resulting in the breaking up of a large percentage of black
households that would be otherwise two-parent homes.*

*From the article
"6 Actual Facts Shatter the Biggest Stereotypes of Black Fathers"
by Antwuan Sargent
www.Mic.com
June 14, 2014*

This generation, I've noticed, there is more Black men involved with their children. We might not be a collective family, but I don't see too many deadbeats. It's far and few between that I see a deadbeat that I associate with or been around. My generation and younger, them dudes is with their kids, hands down. But what we miss is the collective family. There's not a collective community overall, and that's what's hurtin' us in the long run.

DOUGLAS FORT

DOUGLAS FORT, LIKE MANY OF US, wears multiple hats. He is an entrepreneur, community activist, father, husband, sports lover, and well-intentioned representative of his community in East Palo Alto, California. Doug is a multifaceted man.

As an impressionable younger man, Doug got caught up in the street life. Eventually, Doug's choice of lifestyle led to him getting shot.

Doug shed his former life. He then dedicated himself to improving the outcomes of his own life, the lives of his kids, and the lives of youth and young adults in his community. With age, mentorship, and maturity, he was even able to make a strong attempt at securing a seat as a city councilman.

I had the pleasure of gaining insight from Doug. Doug provided candid opinions on topics related to his personal journey through fatherhood. He offered ways to manage having different children by different women. Doug provided the means of becoming a "whole person." Perhaps most importantly, Doug gave info on how he's found success in navigating the dreaded family-court system.

DOUG: I am thirty-seven years old, and I am about to be married. Yes. Very happy about that. My oldest son is named De'Jon Fort. He's fifteen. And my daughter, Zion Fort, she is five. So fifteen and five. I got a little distance between 'em. Boy and a girl.

My kids are kind of self-disciplined. They kind of do their own thing. They figure out somethin' they want to do, and they stay in that lane. So I really ain't had children that I had to deal with on a discipline level or talkin' back or whatever. I kinda just been blessed to have real good children, good people.

I've been blessed that I was raised with a father. My family is kind of a strong, male-oriented family. I know who my biological grandfather is. I met my biological great-grandmother. All my uncles. I was raised around *men*. So those are definitely my primary influences.

But then there is secondary influence. As I walked out of my house, I had Mr. Puckett down the street. I had Mr. Williams around the corner. We had Mr. Goodwin, Mr. Brown, and Mr. Winfrey. I mean, my block was full of men.

And thirdly, when I got into the street life, it was still a male-dominated "sport." So I was raised in a situation where I had nothing but real men around me. It forced me to be one myself. So I was fortunate.

I was fortunate to have that on all three levels: household, secondary in the community, and when I was in the streets as well. And also a fourth level, having spiritual men in my life as well as I got older. All those areas mold me into what I am today.

No excuses. Handle your business. I can hear the conversation right now. "Those *your* babies. *You* made 'em, so handle your business." The loudest thing was just having some integrity. I come from the world of "You're gonna handle your business, and you're gonna man up." That started from inside my house all the way to the streets.

My father is an awesome man. As I look back on it, he's an awesome dude. But growin' up, my father was going through a depression, so he was not as present. Even though he was physically there in my household, he wasn't *present emotionally*. He did what he needed to do to sustain the household, but he was never present. He never helped me with my homework. He never supported me in my football games. 'Cause he was on his own trip. But I understand now what he was goin' through.

I really didn't start getting a relationship with my father until maybe seven, eight years ago. As I got older, we started buildin' and growin' together. Him seeing me as a man and me doin' my thing, we was able to talk about those past pains together. He was able to apologize for his absence. That was a *big* thing for me. I was thirty years old when he first told me he was proud of me. That *changed my whole life*. I'd been lookin' for that. Most boys are lookin' for a father to say, "I'm proud of you, son. Good job."

But see, God is so good. You might have not got it from your father. But I was on the block. So all my homeboys I was hangin' with, they came and supported me at my games. They came and was like, "You ain't gonna miss practice." If I'm short on some money to get some cleats, they copped that.

Dudes I was on the blade with really became my surrogate father. They taught me how to drive a stick. Taught me how to approach a female. Taught me how to defend myself. All the things that Pops didn't give, them dudes on the block gave me. And I'm always respecting that.

Me and my grandfather, we've always had a relationship. Pops is an old playboy. I mean, his personality, a real laid back dude. He used to send for me and my older brother every Christmas. We used to go to L.A. So I've always had a relationship with my grandfather.

I really built a personal relationship with my grandfather when I left to college. I went to go live with him. In that relationship, I learned so many manhood things. He was an OG. He came from the South. And he didn't have no understandin' for shenanigans.

So he taught me hard work, budgeting your money, speakin' up for yourself, being confident of who you are, teachin' me how to hunt properly. He taught me all these manhood things I was supposed to get from my father. Grandpa gave me that.

That's why I said I'm blessed to have a real intimate relationship with my grandfather *and* I have a real intimate relationship with my father. So I'm winnin'. But it wasn't overnight. I was emotionally scarred. And not knowing how to respond. So I fought a lot. Got kicked out of school a lot. I took it out on women. There was a lot of unhealthy things that resulted in the emotional absence of my father. So it wasn't always gravy.

My family is all brilliant people. Like high intellects. So for you to have a conversation with them, you got to come with it. My dad is not gonna listen to no shenanigans. You better come on his level politically, socially, intellectually, all that. They come from that era of intellect.

So I ran for city council of East Palo Alto in 2008. And he [my father] was seeing the work I was puttin' in. All the work I was doin' in the hood. And he was like, "That's *my boy!*" So I think when he saw me grindin' at a level that he understands, that he respects: high intellect, handlin' your business, fightin', and standin' up for something. He's like, "That's my boy!"

That's the reason why I think me and him have been able to bond. Plus, he comes from men. I'm handlin' my business as a man. He's seen me with my son. He's seen me handle my business with my daughter. So he's lookin' like, "This is my boy. He's doin' what Forts do." So I think that when he saw those things he was like, "Okay, I can now have a conversation with my son."

The reason why I ran for city council was because I wanted to show my 'hood that one of us can do something different. Let's get involved. Sharifa Wilson, an OG city councilwoman, said, "If you ain't at the table, you can't eat. You can't make policy, so don't say nothin." And I remembered her saying that when I was a kid. So for me, I'm a doer. My attempt was just to show other people behind me that you can do it too.

I come from a revolutionary city. Nairobi Village, East Palo Alto, was a very strong community, like Oakland. There was a program called Leadership Training Academy. They used to run this summer camp, Community Government Institute, at Stanford [University]. In that, we did a mock city. So that meant you had to run for city council. You had to do your campaign. All these things on a mock level. So I was getting laced up at twelve, thirteen, and fourteen. So running for city council in 2008 wasn't nothing new. I was taught by this behavior by these revolutionary type of teachers in my community.

Coming from the 'hood, you'd be like, "I ain't messin' with the government like that." We don't want to get involved with policing. We don't want to get involved with city council. 'Cause we don't wanna be labeled as a snitch. But that's how you fight. If you wanna dictate change, you gotta be a part of it.

So in that, I ran in 2008 because I wanted the 'hood to see that. That means the old crack dealer. Dude that got shot in the face. In my campaign it was like ex-drug dealer, Douglas Fort. And I wasn't offended. It was true, number one. But number two, that young kid could say, "I was hustlin' too. How can he make it up there?" It wasn't about win, lose, or draw. It was about me showing the people behind me, "You can do this too."

I think one of the things we make a mistake on, just men in general, but as a dad, is being honest with self. Be honest about your feelings. What happens is we mask everything, and we blow up. Blow up on her, on the system, or on anybody else. So be honest about your feelings. That, I think, is number one.

Number two, seek guidance outside of your comfort zone. What happens is, say for instance you and your child's mother is havin' a conflict, and you all involve the court system. Most men, especially men of color, don't wanna go 'cause they are uncomfortable in that arena. And then they don't go seek counsel.

As a young man, having a son—I had him at twenty-one—there are certain things I just couldn't do. I had to sit myself down. I had to do certain things. I had to change a lifestyle. And that means being humbled.

If you could start off with those two [being honest with self and seeking guidance] things get easier as you go through this landscape dealing with your children's mother or your wife. So those qualities are huge. Being honest with self. Then, being a teachable person. If you get those two qualities, you gonna get out your own way. 'Cause most of the time, you'll be in your own way 'cause you're emotional.

You could actually get things done. But you're like, "F that! She shouldn't have did that." And "F her! I'm just not gonna deal with it." I'm gonna run from the situation instead of seeking counsel on the situation and really get things done and benefit the child in the long run.

I made many mistakes. These two things wasn't in the forefront of me at twenty-one, twenty-two, twenty-three years old.

And again, not havin' a relationship with my father because he was goin' through what he was goin' through. Number two, I'm transitioning from the streets too. My relationship with my dudes on the streets ain't what it used to be.

So now I gotta feel comfortable talking to this square cat? He don't know me. You don't know who I am. He don't identify with me. I had to grow out of all that immaturity in fatherhood. And yeah, it's a journey as you walk through because we're fighting our self. That's the number-one fight. It ain't really even *her*. It ain't even the court system.

Crack is a helluva drug. I say heroin took the daddies, crack took the mamas, the War on Drugs took me and your generation, and now the devil himself got our babies. Communities don't exist like they used to when I was growin' up. There is no nuclear family.

It's now all women-driven. And I'm not knockin' the women; they doin' their best. They holdin' it down for us Black men. *We* are the ones that's absent. *We're* the problem.

I'm blessed to have my dad and grandfather. There's some dudes that said, "I've never seen my grandfather. I've never met my dad." That is a chasm. That's a hole. So what examples do they have? They following their mama.

This generation, I've noticed, there is more Black men involved with their children…we might not be a collective family, but I don't see too many deadbeats. It's far and few between that I see a deadbeat that I associate with or been around. My generation and younger, them dudes is with their kids, hands down. But what we miss is the collective family. There's not a collective community overall, and that's what's hurtin' us in the long run. I think the daddy wound, the mama wound, affects women as well.

If you understand the history of America, the Black man is used as an individual to generate income off of. So imagery is that it's easy for you to dehumanize these individuals. If you can dehumanize this individual on TV, when a police officer shoots him or incarcerates him, we can show him as of no value. 'Cause *you had no value back then*. You was a piece of property.

So what we gotta do, as Black men, is put value on self. When we put value on self, we don't act in that fashion. You put some boundaries on yourself, and you won't let nobody exploit you. But at the end of the day, the value of Black men has never been high. On top of that, in urban cities, they're sayin' that we don't value *each other* as Black men anymore. This is why they can get away with [the murder of unarmed Black men by the police]: 'cause we allow it. We don't say anything no more as a collective front.

Another thing we that we need to do is that we have to start preparing our Black kids for this international exchange. Collectively, we have to invest in our babies. And I'm not just talkin' sports. And this can't happen without a collective front. A collective front between me and [Zion's] mother. Her mother sees value in that even though we separated. She's not lettin' her emotions or whatever she has against me supersede that endgame.

What has happened, though, the problem between the mama and the daddy has superseded the endgame with the child. And *he* [the child] loses because we're both emotional. I'm telling you right now, my oldest son's mother is *awesome*. She's a wonderful mother. But my son can do more if *we* were in a communicative conversation. He can be way more awesome if we communicated.

I would *never* take away what she's done for that boy. She's put him in a great school. One of the best schools in the country. Socially and emotionally, how much stronger would he be if me and his mom was not at different viewpoints?

Let's back up a little bit and own *my* side of it. Remember, we gotta talk about honesty? In my walk with her, we had that boy young. And in bein' young, I did young-man things to her to make her dislike me. Rightfully so 'cause I wasn't right. So that created a chasm between me and her. And we went to the courts. We fought in the courts. We did everything under the sun to dislike each other. By the grace of God, our son is healthy.

I had to fight my way from supervised visitations to only getting my son for four hours. This is my son! Saturday and Sunday, for four hours. Twelve p.m. to four. From there, not even seein' him for a year just because of our odds. I'm his biological father, but [the courts] didn't care. But there's ways to beat that [the family-court system].

So for us comin' through the neighborhood, I recommend to these young men we've gotta become a whole person first—spiritually, emotionally, and financially—before you start tryin' to invite your wife and your children.

"Doug, how you do that?" That's the next question. Well, how you become a whole person spiritually? You choose your faith first. If you an Agnostic, roll with it. If you're an Atheist, roll with it. If you're a Christian, a Muslim, roll with it, because that gives you your standard of living, your spiritual level, your foundation. Then, after that, you filter everything through that religion. 'Cause then you'll know just how emotionally you can use it. And then go find men in that world to help you get through these emotional situations.

Once you find who you are as in buildin' the whole person, everything else is gonna fall into place. You gonna know your role. You gonna be able to say no. You will even value yourself even more.

As a young man, I made mistakes because I wasn't a whole person. Once you become whole, life changes. Your value system changes. Everything changes. You can work on yourself as young as possible.

I was kind of blessed because I had my children after I got my degree. I was in a situation where financially I was gonna get money. So for the young cat that's havin' it at seventeen, eighteen years old, it's gonna be difficult because he gotta *find* money. I was blessed to have that foundation of having an undergraduate degree. And then I'm able to apply and make significant, career money. So secure your finances first, if you can.

If you got multiple baby mamas, such as myself, I recommend for you to be cool with that mate. Let me break down that relationship balance. *Stop playin' with these women.* What happens is you wanna play with her on all levels. You still wanna hit it on the low. Then you wanna have your fun over there. Then you hatin' on the new dude that comes. That's drama. You gotta set boundaries. If it's over, homie, it's over, homie. And you move on, and y'all focus on building Team Whatever-Your-Child's-Name-Is. Like I told you with my daughter, it's *Team Zion*. We're done. Ain't nothin' happenin'.

What happens, us bein' young, we still tryin', we flippin', floppin', and playin' games. That's our number-one problem. You still tryin' to get lost in the sauce. You tryin' to have a good time. And hey, I'm a victim of it myself.

But what happens is that I made her believe something that didn't exist. And when she found out, she became *bitter*. She became a scorned woman and ready to cut my head off because I played her. So if you're not gonna be together, you gonna have to act strong enough and move on.

Number two, you gotta work on a team schedule. Don't play games because you really wanna run off with the fellas or be with this little second piece. You prioritize the time that you have with your kid. Then you act a fool on the times when you don't. But when it's time for you and your kid, shut that down. That takes discipline. Requires you to be a whole person.

Now if she catch feelings, you ain't got nothin' to do with that. But as long as you ain't creating it. If you as an individual are dealing with these multiple women, you're in a situation where you control your own destiny. It's about puttin' boundaries up. Then a financial plan and a visitation plan for your kids. And follow it. You do that, you ain't gotta see the man in the courtroom, period. But *you the lead* in that. You gonna have to learn how to navigate that.

When you have a child with somebody, you built the intimacy. You built a relationship with her. It's hard to break away from bein' intimate with this person. So let me be realistic to these young players. It's hard not to be engaged and you still physically attracted, but the relationship is over. But that's the whole-person part. You gotta put strong men around you for that sound counsel so you can run those ideas toward your sound counsel.

Say, for instance, you got kids with one. And she's just havin' taco night. Your daughter or son may say, "I wanna see my dad." You ain't got nothin' else to do. You swing through after work. Y'all have taco night. Everything's cool. But y'all had a brew, some wine, and there it goes again. But y'all been removed from each other four, five months. Then y'all get into that situation over again. That's where the drama comes. We gotta tear it *all the way* off. For me, the best thing that ever happened to me was to make my yes, *my yes* and my no, *my no.*

One of the things is that we don't talk among men. We might shuck 'n' jive about the Laker game, but we don't really talk about this hard, emotional stuff. This stuff is *hurtful.* It's stuff we're not taught to talk about. And I felt compelled to do it because I've been there and done that. So I'm speakin' to it. I'm tryin' to give life to that young cat or whoever is goin' through it now so that they can come up out of it.

And let's talk about this courtroom for a minute. You can beat it if you stay patient. If you meet the mandate of that [court] schedule, it's gonna increase your visitations. But some of us don't have the patience or the guidance around you to soothe you on that time when you gotta be there only twelve to four. Or when she's playin' with you and she don't show up to the drop-off. Or when you gotta go get the police to help you get your son to enforce the court order. Be patient. Be diligent. The courts are forced to look at your track record and increase your visitation. So my advice to young men is to come in there with a plan.

Another thing that we don't do is that we don't write down the incidents where she is playing with the kids. If she don't show up to the visitation, write that day and time down. Because in that courtroom she's gonna have to answer why weren't you there?

You gotta learn the system. Learn it, and learn how to compete in it so in the long run you can win. I was able to get my son half time because of me being patient in that courtroom. So you gonna either win this game or not. Get up out of your feelings. Go get some guidance so you can maintain and go get your youngster. At the end of the day, *you* are responsible for him.

The state of California mandates what your percentage is. If you got one kid, twenty-five percent of your income goes to that kid. If you got two kids, forty percent of your income goes to that kid. Three kids or more, it's fifty percent. That means even if you have no visitations, they smack you for a quarter of your income. So you *gotta* go get your son, or they're gonna take a quarter of your money regardless. So in that, it's putting brothas in a situation. This system is not designed for you to be successful. I got fifteen years of experience to tell.

You can beat the court system if you stay patient and you do what they ask you to do. Once you do all the mandates, they *gotta* increase [your visitation rights].

My son, I'm proud of that dude. He's a stand-up dude. I see the things that I've taught him being manifest today. Just making his word his word. Following through about what he's doin'. He's just taken pride in being a young man. His football team made him the captain. They went to the coach and made him captain. So that's tellin' me that your peer group sees you as the man. It relates to leadership.

As I was raising him, because we're visual men, you could talk to your son all day or your daughter all day, but they wanna see it. You don't have to say much. My dad didn't say much. But I seen him cook dinner every night. That's why I know how to cook dinner. I seen him sit at the table and make bills. That's how I pay my bills. I was able to see it.

My kids takin' pride in what they like is my blessing. They livin' a good life. They laugh, and they havin' a good time. Daddy's straight. They straight. I'm straight.

[I'm most proud of myself for] Growing from an emotional weenie to an emotional warrior. From weak spiritually to strong spiritually. These things will test you. This relationship with the girl and your children and these courts will test who you are. And I feel comfortable because I stayed down. I was able to take these hits. I took a lot of hits. So for me, I'm proud of stayin' down and never compromising who I was or who I am. It was some lows. But at the high of it, I don't feel uncomfortable at all.

So as a Black man that's *in love with Black people*, I understand the pressures that we have. But you become a whole man, and then you gonna make your kid a whole person too.

Eric Handy
"Two Sides to a Story"

*A child points out to you the direction,
and then you find your way.*

Luhya (Kenya, East Africa) Proverb

I don't want that for my life. I choose to make the
sacrifices and the choices that's gonna help me prevent
my kids from experiencing or seeing or living or
enduring some of the hurt that I have endured.

ERIC HANDY

ERIC JAY HANDY IS A young man of reinvention. He's a chameleon—able to change, adapt, and succeed in numerous scenarios. Over the years, Eric has juggled the tasks of being a party promoter and event planner. On top of that, he's been a professional educator, in charge of coordinating St. Mary's College of California's High Potential Program. Simultaneously, he's been the program director for the Lincoln Child Center's Oakland Freedom Schools.

Meanwhile, Eric has managed to complete his undergraduate and master's degrees in recent years. To put some icing on the cake, he's remained a dedicated husband and father of three. Needless to say, Eric can offer up some advice on balancing life, higher education, and professional goals all while remaining true to family.

ERIC: My name is Eric Jay Handy. I am thirty-five. My children, the eldest, is ten, Jalen Andrew Handy. My middle child is seven, Tatiana Rose Handy. And then my youngest child is three, Aidan Eric Jay Handy.

And you're absolutely correct. They are experiencing life in different stages. And although they may be sharing in the same experiences, being in the same household, the way they're projecting that experience, the way it's being manifested, because of their ages, provides a Pandora's Box of situations. Emotions. It's always a fun roller coaster, though.

And without sounding gender-biased, I do believe, in my personal parental preference, that I do parent my boys differently than I parent my girl. I *only have one girl*. When Aidan first came along, Tatiana was three. She was really jealous. She didn't really like it because she was going from the youngest to, now, the middle child. Her roles were shifting. She had a hard time. She really grappled with accepting responsibility as an older sister. Whereas Jaelan always embraced his role as the eldest, the older sibling. Even to this day he's very conscious of taking care of his younger sister and brother.

From my perspective and my experience, I don't know what an ideal father is. I grew up raised predominantly by women. It was really my Auntie Gwen, my Auntie Sheila, and my Auntie Denise, and my Auntie Glenna, who still to this day are the matriarchal and patriarchal figure.

My grandmother was a single mother. All of my aunties were single mothers, for the most part. All of my uncles, at some point in their lifetime, were absentee fathers. So when you ask me, "What does the ideal father look like?" My initial response would be Cliff Huxtable. Or P. Diddy. I don't know. A good Tupac song? I don't know what a good example of fatherhood is.

I know what I *don't* want to be. And I know how I *don't* want to act. I know what it's like to be a fourteen year-old boy who is living with his auntie who has four kids of her own. And she's a single mother. Basically being a surrogate mother to endless cousins, nephews, and nieces.

And that same fourteen-year-old boy doesn't even have anybody in the house, other than his eldest cousin, to teach him how to shave. Or has another family member have to teach him how to box because he's being bullied. And so I don't want that for my sons. I know what it's like for a young girl who's been raped and is looking for a father figure because her father's gone, out of her life. I don't want that for my daughter.

I don't want that for my life. I choose to make the sacrifices and the choices that's gonna help me prevent my kids from experiencing or seeing or living or enduring some of the hurt that I have endured.

My grandmother was a single mother. All her kids were single parents. I'm basically saying that everybody I seen was a single parent.

When I found out I was going to be a dad, I was scared for my life. And I was tired of having abortions. It didn't really hit me at first. I was chillin'. I was turnin' up. I was doin' my life.

I was at a good friend's golden-glove boxing tournament in San Francisco. I went to the bathroom. And as I walked in the bathroom, there was a gentleman and his son who couldn't have been more than three. He was teaching his son how to use the urinal. I was just washing my hands, and I was just gazed in on them. It just stopped me in my tracks. You could tell it was a real proud father moment for him.

And when he left the bathroom, I cried. 'Cause I was scared at that point. I was having my first son. I was half employed. I was just starting school all over again. I didn't know what it was gonna be with this lady (wife, Andrea). I was kind of feeling pressure to have this kid. And I *didn't want to be my father*. And so in that moment, I was scared. I was really scared. I'll never forget that moment. I was scared of not being able to make the right choices which may leave me absent from my son's life. I didn't want that.

My mom had my older brother when she was sixteen. She had me at twenty-one. I was an adult when I first realized that my mother was twenty-one and my father was *thirty-nine* when I was born. My father was a grown man, right?

So for Christmas vacation, I'm two or three, she took me and my brother for a visit to Texas. I never saw my father again until 1999. From age three, 1983 to 1999, I didn't know who my father was. I never saw my father. I just heard stories about my father. They were never good. They were never positive.

So that's what I was most afraid of. It wasn't like my father was in jail. It wasn't like my father was dead. He was alive in the streets *in the same city that I was in.* And I didn't see my father for that whole time.

My mom's family, they were struggling to make ends meet. I never lived in a house where I wasn't conscious and aware that the lights could not be on today. There's probably not gonna be nothing to eat in the refrigerator. You got to find your own way from A to B. Wearing hand-me-downs. So my childhood has affected my fatherhood in a way that my sole desire is to get to a level where that's not an issue for my children.

Additionally, build a family structure where they're not worried about them not being loved emotionally or psychologically. I'm much more aware. I'm acutely aware of my children's needs because I was so in need as a child. So I'm always thinking about their needs and projecting their needs, trying to intentionally shape my life as such.

I think emotional support is definitely important. Being present, and what the heart hears. It's important to be present, not just physically, but mentally. So I am very emotionally aware of what my children are going through. I talk to my children all the time. I'm much more of a conversationalist than I am a punishment type of guy.

Before you have kids, if you have the choice, really be intentional about getting your career off the ground. Get your education up. Get your career going. Find your spiritual balance. It's been extremely difficult to do what I've done. Not everybody can do it. And I've been blessed to have a very strong support system. My mother-in law to my mom to aunties to uncles to cousins to friends to neighbors. Community who just help and support my efforts and endeavors.

Ever since I've had kids, I've dropped them off to school. That's been the routine. That's been something I've been near and dear, dedicated to. I've taken real pride in taking my kids to school. But I'd drop my kids off, and then I would go to work.

Then I would go to school at night. So I would be putting in twelve, fourteen-hour days. I would come home and try to do a little bit of the night routine: pick up, wash dishes, clean up, iron, and pack lunches. *Then* I would hit the computer for another three more hours. I wouldn't get to bed 'til two in the morning. Then wake up at five, and do it all over again. So the best advice is you *gotta* get a strong support system 'cause it's not easy.

The male role is to be the lead. And lead doesn't mean that you have to be the first. But being the male role, we're the spearhead. The Black man's role, when you go into the community, no matter if you're the janitor, you're the principal, you're the student, you're the father, you have to exemplify what *our* culture is. You have to model it. So the role of the Black man, as a father or as an educator or anything else in the community, is to be that pillar of representation. We are the example. Whenever an African American man moves and integrates into a different profession, they become automatically a pillar in that profession. We excel. That's what we do. That's where our heritage comes from.

As I worked for Freedom School, I saw fathers there dropping their sons or daughters off and picking them up every day. I see fathers staying, waiting, asking questions, wanting to talk to the teachers, saying, "Hey, I'm concerned about the education my daughter or son's getting. Hey, I'm concerned about what's going on in our community."

The troubling aspect of that is that young boys and girls in our community, they are only buying into what they see popularized by social media and television. Popular media of today glorifies the negative aspects of our African American community. It objectifies the negative aspects of what a Black man or woman is. That negates all the hard work that real African American fathers are doing in the community.

I grew up on hip-hop. Hip-hop raised me. I'm a hip-hop head. I love going to different concerts. I loved Tupac. I love Too $hort. One of my good friends is a hip-hop artist, Mistah F.A.B. He's an exceptional father, by the way.

I just think there's a medium, a place for the music of hip-hop that is right for your children. It can uplift the Black community and Black fatherhood. There's a plethora of artists that do speak life through hip-hop. I just choose to infuse my children with those musicians' music.

I mean, thank God for Barack Obama because he broke that glass ceiling. They used to say, "You could be anything, Eric. You could be President one day." I realized quickly that they were lying to me. Now we know that it is feasible. History has proven it is feasible. People are getting fed so much garbage (through media). So as a Black man, we got to be the vegetables. We got to be that protein because they're getting fed so much carbs, so much saturated fat all the time.

President Obama's image speaks volumes. I believe it illustrates, through example, what the Black man is and what the Black community, and other communities, have already known the Black man is.

For years, the highest depiction that Western society has given us of a Black man has been Martin Luther King. They said Martin Luther King was the greatest. But they never really talk about Martin Luther King being a father. There's very few books that articulate just how much of a father he was and what that meant to Western society.

The President, Barack Obama, it's not by happenstance that you do see him coming off from his recent vacation with his oldest daughter Malia. It speaks volumes that there's a President in the office that's Black that is illustrating how to be a real father.

The pride and ego in me would like to do a Derek Luke, to go and do an Antoine Fisher. Like, "You know, I ain't never smoked or drank! I'm a man. I've been in the army!" And kind of just say, "Look, you left me, and look how well I turned out!" I would *love* to do that to my father. But the God in me, at this point, would just want to be in his presence. Just soak up any wisdom I could, actually.

It was New Year's Eve, 1999. I was on my way to East Faith Deliverance Church. I had on a black leather coat, a red-and-black shirt from Eddie Bauer. Had some Gap jeans. And some red-and-black Jordans on. I'll never forget it. I thought I was so fly. And I walked in there to go see Enoch Handy. That's where it was rumored he was gonna be.

Now, you know, I thought the world was going to end. Everybody thought the world was going to end in 2000. So I was like, "Well, if the world's gonna end, at least I should go see my father before it ends."

And it was like a scene out of a movie, and I'll never forget it. I could see it as clear as day. I walked through this long corridor. The lights were kind of out, so it was really dark. There was just a glimmer of light coming from the end at the corner to my right. It was real cold and sterile. And to the left there was a small opening. In the opening was a carpet and an organ and a mirror. And he was back there playing the organ.

I just stood in the hallway, kind of just looking at him for a moment or two. It felt like an eternity to me. And he was like, "Are you lost? Can I help you?" And I was like, "Do you even know who I am?"

And he got up and walked to the kitchen. Walked right past me. Still with his back to me. He was like, "Yeah, I know who you are." The first words out of his mouth—I'll never forget—was, "There's always two sides to a story."

I was very arrogant, not as humble as I am now. Didn't have much wisdom. So I was mad. Like "I don't want to hear about no two sides of a story. You owe me!" I was in there looking for some sense of entitlement, right? Those words rang hollow. They stick with me and echo. "There's two sides to a story."

Jay-Z dropped an album, *The Magna Carta Holy Grail.* And at the end of the album he has a song that's called "Daddy Dearest." And it's a song to his daughter. And he says, "If it was up to me, you would be with me, sort of like Daddy Dearest." I listen to that song whenever I'm having a hard time being a father or a husband or being a parent.

And I think about that one instance that I had with my father. It *is two sides* to a story. And I don't want to have to be on the other end of that story or on the other end of that Jay-Z song, saying to my kids, "Man, if it was up to me, you would be with me."

So I use that experience as a motivation to really take it on the chin. You know, to keep my nose to the grindstone. To keep bettering myself. To do what I have to do to be consistent in my kids' lives. And to empower myself to be in a better position so I am actively participating in my kids' lives.

Dr. Steven Millner
"Knowledge, Wisdom and Lessons from Dr. Millner"

Children learn more from what you are than what you teach.

W. E. B. Du Bois

*Love your children like the gems they are. If you don't treasure
your children, how can you expect others to treasure your children?*

DR. STEVEN MILLNER

A ROLE MODEL, MENTOR, FATHER and father figure, historian, master storyteller, sociologist, and educator, Dr. Steven Millner has enjoyed a successful professional career in higher education for over forty years. Dr. Millner may have even been able to enjoy a successful career in comedy, as he has an incredible sense of humor and good comedic timing. Just ask the thousands of young adults whom he's taught, led, and interacted with over the last four decades. He is a pillar in Bay Area higher education. A memorable man. One of those teachers who leaves a lasting impression. Everyone always remembers the days when they took Dr. Millner's classes.

Perhaps most importantly, Dr. Steven Millner has been both a husband and father of three children for more than forty years. Personally, Dr. Millner has survived serious health issues. Professionally, he's survived statewide attacks on Ethnic Studies departments. Finally, he's survived what he considers the BC and AC generations—meaning *Before Crack* and *After Crack*. Dr. Millner was able to provide a great narrative on fatherhood, responsibility, and lessons he's learned throughout his life.

STEVEN: I'm Steven Millner. I'm a professor of African American studies and history at San Jose State University. And a father since I was twenty-one years old. I have three children. My oldest daughter's a university graduate from Cal-Poly and the mother of my only grandson. My son, who's a Stanford-trained lawyer. Then my daughter, who's a Harvard graduate. And I've been married for forty-two and a half years.

But I am also the son of a father who was married to my mother for forty-nine years. And my grandfather was married to my grandmother for forty-five years. So being a father is a family tradition. And being a husband, being involved in those kinds of family dynamics, is part of the Millner, Johnson, Scott legacy.

And in those forty-two years we may have been through eight or nine separations. But reconciliations always took place. We haven't had a separation in more than twenty years. But those early years were real tough 'cause we got married in Berkeley in the 1970s. Nobody in our generation was doing that kind of traditional, matrimony, marriage thing. It's as much of a testament to my wife's patience and her love as it is to my connection to the idea that you're not a *real man*, at least from our family's point of view, unless you father children and do right by them.

So I designed my career. Being a professor, I had flexibility of scheduling. I could always take my children to school in the morning. And by being the driver to take them in the morning and being the pickup parent in the afternoon, it allowed me to impart to my children the importance of education.

My kids saw me graduate with a master's and doctorate from UC Berkeley in my twenties and thirties. They were seeing me do what I was telling them to do and what I expected from them. It was leadership through example.

One of the things that really motivated me as a young man and reinforced how I approach my life was Daniel Patrick Moynihan's scathing denunciation of the collapse of the Black family in 1960. I took that personal. That *did not* describe the kind of family situation that I had. It was a scathing indictment of Black men in particular.

Moynihan said that Black men's habits were based on promiscuity. We were unwilling to be the backbone of our families. And I was personally affronted by that. It certainly didn't describe the father I knew. It didn't describe my grandfathers. It didn't describe the things I had seen in my community. I was insulted! He painted us as Black men with a negative, broad brush.

Being the son of a postman and hearing my dad get up every morning at four thirty a.m. and struggle to go to work in the Columbus, Ohio, wintertime. Him being persistent. Walking seven miles, nine miles, in the snow. It just reminded me that you're really not a man unless you do the things to protect your own. It was crystal clear that if we didn't protect our own, White society *and* Negro society would eat folks up.

What was really important to see was that my dad worked, and he wore a uniform. He wore a postal employee uniform, and he took pride in that. I immediately began to note that work was what a man was *supposed to do.* You came home from work, you changed your clothes, and then you lived a life with your children. My dad's life revolved around going to work in the morning, coming home in the afternoon, and then spending his time with his four sons and his daughter. He spent a lot more time with his sons than his daughter because that was just the way of life in the fifties.

We had all these family rituals. Just a rites of passage. You got a single-shot twenty-two when you were twelve. You got a twenty-gauge shotgun when you were fourteen. You got a sixteen-gauge double-barrel shotgun when you were sixteen. And we all hunted together; my father, his brother, my uncle's sons. We were going out to the Ohio fields putting meat on the table. We were expected to do that. That's the kind of legacy that we had. Men coming of age whose ethnicity was not just African American but also Native American. My dad always took pride in the fact that one of his grandmothers was a full-blooded Cherokee.

With the five of us, we always ate dinner together at six o'clock. My oldest brother would always have to report what he had done in school that day. Then, after he reported what he had learned, my other brother would report on what he had learned. Then it would be my turn. So by listening to the reports and giving the reports, the value of education was always reinforced night after night. As I look back at it, I now understand that was very rare. But it was really the strength of these family rituals that got us through.

But my dad had all the frustrations of being a Black man in America. He had not been able to graduate from Ohio State University, and he always regretted that. So he *always* preached the virtue of getting your education finished. And we, his kids, took that to heart. In fact, he moved us to California, from Ohio, with the goal of getting us in a location where all five of his children could go to a university.

In the sixties California didn't charge tuition at the state university or UC level. All five of us went through the UC and CSU systems in the 1960s without paying tuition. But my parents made a great sacrifice to move us to California because they had no family here. My mom and dad met at Ohio State. Neither of them had the resources to finish.

My mother was a frustrated dropout. She wanted to be a teacher. She'd been a straight-A student. Her mother had been a teacher in a one-room classroom down in a rural community. We had that kind of ethic reinforced. Our teachers always told us, "You're gonna have to be twice as good to get half as much." And it was true.

When I left LA County to go to college and got away from my personal family rituals, I began to see the kinds of attitudes and behaviors and values that people from outside of my family expressed so openly. I was aghast. I was appalled. I saw guys who had the hustler mentality with women as creatures that they were supposed to exploit.

I was here at San Jose State University in the late sixties when this hustlin' mentality was in high operation. The "free love" generation was so pervasive in the Bay Area in the late sixties. The access to all kinds of drugs in the late sixties. I saw that tear folks up! I mean literally just destroy people.

It's really apparent to me that I was coming of age in the last era before modern technology in a variety of ways transformed life around the globe. By the time I left home at age twenty and moved to the Bay Area, *everything* was breaking wide open. I watched the casualties.

I was in a dorm suite at Joe West Hall at San Jose State. Eight other guys in the suite. One of 'em ended up killing a cop. He had all kinds of psychiatric issues. Killing a cop on Tenth and Santa Clara Streets, in 1971. And he's doing life. Never gonna walk free. One of the other guys from that suite ended up committing suicide after getting drafted to the military. Two of the other guys ended up dying in the 1980s of HIV/AIDS.

So I saw the kind of shattering experiences that young Black men from my immediate generation went through. But it especially turned sinister in the late seventies, early eighties, when crack began to replace bud, weed, as the drug of choice. I watched that with horror.

Within two to three years there were crack houses up and down the street where my mom and dad were living. Because we had been raised with the kind of skills my father had imparted, we brothers would take turns on the weekend essentially standing guard at my mama's house so that the crack heads and the crack trade wouldn't engulf my mom's house. The drive-bys and things like that were beginning to proliferate.

And when the crack thing hit big in LA County and here in the Bay Area, where it was ground zero, it was *horrific*. I saw young women that I had gone to high school with turn into "strawberry girls" who would do anything to get that next hit of crack. And it's been downhill ever since, in many respects. But every generation has its challenges.

When cities like Detroit and Chicago lost hundreds of thousands of jobs with the mechanization of factories, Black men were left unemployed. When Detroit had its collapse in the seventies, all those Black families in Detroit, the men had no real alternatives to turn to. So they turned to what was available. And that was the underground economy. I was sophisticated enough to understand what was happening, but I couldn't change the American economy. And I understood why people would turn to any means necessary to survive.

It's a dog-eat-dog world out there. And the drugs, especially drugs like cocaine, make people paranoid. And in the eighties you have the consequences of the post-Vietnam generation. More guns and more people equipped to know how to use 'em than at any other time in America's evolution.

We have to remember, African American males were four to five times as likely to be drafted and sent into combat. We're talking about hundreds of thousands of guys who came back, many times embittered and also addicted to drugs. But also skilled and proficient in the use of weapons. The war machine of the sixties and seventies produced more weapons than the world has ever had, and they flooded into lower-class communities. It's just been a vicious, vicious evolutionary cycle.

[Fathers must] Love your children like the gems that they are. If you don't treasure your children, how can you expect others to treasure your children? Your children are *you*. That's what I was led to embrace by my father and my grandfathers. That's exactly what I've inculcated in my children. You are a reflection of your whole family lineage. That's what's important. In many respects, that's been lost across class and race lines. But that's the private ethic I live with.

I've been very protective of my daughters. I spent a lot of time in a frat house, so I know where young guys are coming from. So I impart that kind of knowledge to both of my daughters to protect them. If you love your daughters like I do, you want to protect them from anything that can come their way. I've seen a lot of stuff come in the direction of women. And so definitely, I've had a double standard.

But I also raised my son to be one of a hundred young, Black, male, Eagle Scouts in America in the last twenty or thirty years. And for him to be an Eagle Scout, it meant that I was deeply involved in the whole Boy Scout experience. It was like raising my son in the fields and doing things outdoors like I had been raised to do.

And when I get in the classroom, I'm always thinking that these kids have parents who love them and who are concerned and worried about them. I'm definitely a father figure. I keep my social distance from them. That's why I call them by Mr. and Miss in class. I want them to think of themselves as grown adults and people that I hold responsible for behaving as young adults.

Dr. Sydney Sukuta
"Truly African American"

*The family is the solution to the world's problems
today…in the family, the father is like the head, the
leader, the director, not domineering but showing
love, guidance for everyone else in the family.
If we can get all the fathers in the world to stand
up and be fathers, that would be great.*

The O'Jays, "Family Reunion," 1975

*I think what has happened between the Continental African
and the African American is that we have learned about
each other through the eyes of other people. We are told about
you by other people. You are told about us by other people.
One of the worst things is not to communicate with each
other and let other people communicate in between us.*

D<small>R</small>. S<small>YDNEY</small> S<small>UKUTA</small>

D<small>R</small>. S<small>YDNEY</small> S<small>UKUTA</small> IS A highly esteemed professor of laser technology and physics at a premier institution for higher education in the Silicon Valley. Since 2001,
Sydney has been educating The Valley's young men and women and enabling
them to compete in the cutting-edge, fast-paced, and lucrative high-tech world.

Born and raised in the Mt. Silinda area of Zimbabwe, Sydney is one of
the seven children of the late Mr. Mutengani and Mrs. Kate Sukuta. Recently,
Sydney and his mother helped to chronicle the Sukuta family legacy as founding members of the United Church of Christ in Zimbabwe. In 2014, Sydney
and his mother wrote the autobiographical book *Precious Mt. Silinda: A Century
of African Transformation.* The book details the impact of missionary activity
on his native Zimbabwe. *Precious Mt. Silinda* also serves to detail the impact
and influence of Sydney's parents and grandparents in Mt. Silinda, Zimbabwe.

In 1979, Sydney left Zimbabwe to pursue higher education. Meanwhile,
as a nation, Zimbabwe was negotiating talks to gain its political independence
from England, which it did in 1980. Sydney arrived in England after receiving
a full academic scholarship from the British Council. In 1983, Sydney arrived
in the USA. He studied at the University of Arizona, completing his bachelor's
degree in physics.

A multifaceted and multilingual man, who's come a long way from precious
Mt. Silinda, Sydney occupies many unique statuses, depending on the day of
the week. He is a noted Professor. He's an author. Sydney is also gifted musician.
Among all else, he's a husband and father of fraternal twins. His son, Sydney
Ten'ani Sukuta and daughter Sydaira Rose Sukuta are both six years old.

Sydney detailed his reasons for authoring the book, *Precious Mt. Silinda*. He offered insight on life growing up in Zimbabwe. And Sydney provided his take on instilling the cultural values of his homeland into his children, as they grow up in the United States.

As a continental African man from Zimbabwe who's married to an African American woman (Sandra Sukuta), Dr. Sydney Sukuta can rightfully say that he is truly African American.

SYDNEY: There are multiple reasons why my mother and I came together to create *Precious Mt. Silinda*. One of them is just as an autobiographical account of my mother and her career and her parents. Just a chronology of the family mostly. Stemming around the time when the mission was founded, 1893. Mt. Silinda Mission, it's a congregational mission. So basically it's a history of the missionary activity where I came from: Mt. Silinda, Zimbabwe.

Both my grandparents and parents were involved with this institution. 1893, that's when my grandparents met the founding missionaries of Mt. Silinda Mission. That became the nucleus of the United Church of Christ in Zimbabwe today. I'm a link to our history for my children. I need to write this down so they can have a reference. It's our duty and responsibility to let the future generations know about their past. Everybody needs to understand who they are, and this is one way to do it.

When I go to the original script, I was still in graduate school. I guess the last five years, that's when I really sat down to finish it up because my mom was here. She was staying in my home for the last nine years in Reno, Nevada. She just went back to Zimbabwe in 2013. The last five years were really critical in getting it done. I was living in Reno at the time, commuting back there on weekends. Then she and I would sit down and get it done. I'd come back and forth between San Jose and Reno.

So it was a slow process. But most importantly, I wanted the book to be as accurate and as detailed as possible. It took quite a good five years. But I guess that's well worth it in terms of the return on your investment.

For me, it was a learning process. I was pretty much transcribing what my mother told me, so I learned a lot. The more I understood, I just felt more comfortable with myself. Some people, I'm sure, they'll find a lot about their ancestors from that book. For us it's more personal. But we touched on other people's ancestors who were participants in the mission-building process in Zimbabwe.

My father, Mutengani, the name is sort of a Zulu type because our people are impacted by the Zulu migrations. Mutengani means "the purchaser" or "the buyer." For me as a child, I think he was very different from other fathers, actually. He was never moody. He was always rational and calm. He was very empathetic. If something good happens for you, then he'll be happy for you that you met your goals.

So as a child, he trusted me a lot. And as I look back, that was very helpful for me. He gave me little projects to do on the farm. He'd ask me things like, "What do you think we should grow here?" So it made me feel like my thoughts and feelings matter to him. And he trusted my judgment. So I think it was very important for me to build my self-esteem in that way.

His empathy, him trusting in my abilities to make decisions at a young age, that impacted everybody's life. That was very important for me. Even to this day, I don't doubt myself much because of that trust. Trust from somebody you respect a lot is very important. As I grew up, at some point, I think we almost were more like friends. Like my older friend!

I remember when he was sick back in Zimbabwe. I said, "You know what, dad? I'm gonna quit everything and come back home." At the time, I was already here in the States working on my bachelor's degree. He said, "Hey, son, keep going. Keep going." He understood the need for me to continue moving forward with my life. Eventually,

I took a semester off to go see him in Zimbabwe and hang out. That was back in '84.

Hanging out with him in Zimbabwe as an adult was pretty cool. Actually, this was about the time the idea of the book *Precious Mt. Silinda* came up. He'd be talking a lot about his own growing up, stories about his own dad to me. I was like, "I need to write these things down at some point." My mom would do the same thing with me. So it was a few years down the road that I actually decided to write it all down.

I'd left Zimbabwe to go to England back in about 1979, '80. In fact, I left Rhodesia in the very last year of Rhodesia's existence to go to England. So I've been absent from day-to-day Zimbabwe culture for over thirty years now. I've spent more time out of Zimbabwe. More than half my life has been outside. So I've transformed in many ways.

So the England thing was I got a scholarship from the British Council when I was seventeen. It covered everything: room, board, and airfare. I just went home and told my parents, "I'm outta here." So September 8, 1979, I flew to England. The country Zimbabwe, at the time, they were actually having talks on negotiations on the independence of the nation, which succeeded. Rhodesia was a British colony.

So Zimbabwe came to fruition in 1980. The scholarships we got were based on the fact that we were living under a very unhealthy political climate. So as soon as the political climate changed, they terminated the scholarships. So that's what basically led me to America.

I wound up at the University of Arizona in 1983. I started off studying electrical engineering and then transitioned to physics. I got my BS degree in physics in the late eighties. In the early nineties I went to Fresno State University, where I got my master's degree in physics. And then about 1993 or so I wound up at the University of Nevada, Reno where I got a PhD in chemical physics.

I think, overall, at the end of the day, integrity's important. And you *need* to practice what you preach. It's important to tell your children the right things, the things *you* believe in and then *practice them.* If you become a hypocrite, when they find out, you go from top ten to minus ten right away.

Be as noble as you can. Pick the right values because for children, their first heroes are their parents. My son was saying, "Daddy, I know you can fix anything!" So I'm his first hero. He believes in me. So for them to see down the road, "That man wasn't all that honest with me," is very damaging. Whatever you do, they're watching you. Whatever you do, they'll do blindly. So I try to be honest.

America, I have lots of respect for this culture. I was *not born* in this culture, necessarily. I *do* understand it. But obviously, my beliefs are rooted in where I came from. I'm not very disappointed in the way that I was raised. So I don't see why I should change it.

Obviously, culturally, there are a lot of differences. The social conduct, just the way people relate to each other compared to where I come from. Clearly I'm coming from an African culture. So in Europe and then in America, there's some cultural differences there. But you know, I try to adapt as much as I can. You know, go with what your hosts do, right?

I don't necessarily agree with all that's happening. But there are times to just follow the rules of your hosts. I think that's one way to get along with people without imposing your opinion. You can tell them "This is the way *I* do it." But you can't impose your wishes everywhere.

There are some things I may disagree with coming from back home too. So the idea is to hybridize the good from both cultures. I live with *both cultures* now.

It's not, "Because it's American, let's not do it." If it's a good thing, let's do it. It's not necessarily because it's African it has to be. At least for my kids, down the road, I don't want to plant any seeds of self-destruction. I have to weed out the bad influences from *both* cultures. That's how I want to raise my kids.

I have tried to stay connected to my own roots by engaging myself in activities that keep me connected with my family, my homeland and culture. Associating with other people from Zimbabwe. In particular, my family and the friends I grew up with are still important. In this high-tech era, we now exchange messages and information almost on a daily basis through these Internet apps. I also immerse myself in my culture by supporting artists in Zimbabwe, Africa, and all Afrocentric cultures through the promotion of the arts. This makes me stay and feel intimately connected to my culture. I hope to pass this on to my children as they come of age.

My kids are definitely Americans. And my wife is African American. So it's about *negotiation*. Every culture experiences some similar things. It really lies in how we handle those things. My wife, she brings her point of view, and we negotiate and strike a balance. So either it's a hybrid approach, or it's her *African American* way.

As things arise, I may say "You know what? I think the way we handled this back home in Zimbabwe wasn't right. I like the African American way," or something neutral, in the middle. But it's important for spiritual and emotional stability and balance to understand yourself. Hold onto your roots. I really want my kids to understand that.

So I try to teach them traditional African values through song—special family songs. We sing a lot of those. Knowing the ancestry, knowing the cultural values I teach them through song, they are exposed to Zimbabwean roots. We sing together in my language, chiNdau. Then some of it I translate to them in English. So kinship is important.

Spiritual balance is important. Belief in a higher power. I want my kids to understand the African ways. But that also helps them to *understand me*. They need to understand where I'm coming from. Kinship, spirituality, gender identification, knowing who you are. Those are what I call *immutable* divine attributes. You need to be able to accept who you are *totally*.

Your racial identity is important. Your gender is important. Your spirituality is important. Once you understand that, you understand *you* better. This is how our higher power made me. So I need to respect that. Once you get that together, the energy or the passion you have can now be invested in excelling in life. So again, knowing yourself, both the African and American parts of who they are, accepting their family, their racial identity is very important.

My wife and I recognize that they are Americans. They were born here. They're being raised here. The whole Zimbabwe thing is really me. They've never been there. But I want them to understand that this is probably one of the greatest countries to be born and raised in. There's a lot of opportunities that can be used to your advantage.

It's a great culture, and I admire African Americans' fortitude. Men like Dr. Martin Luther King, Jr. I and other Africans learned a lot from him. The contributions of African Americans to the general American culture needs to be more recognized. I don't think they are recognized enough. This is the America that African Americans helped put together. African Americans helped *build this country*. Because my kids' heritage is African American, they are a part of these great contributions too.

I think what has happened between the Continental African and the African American is that we have learned about each other through the eyes of *other people*. We are told about *you* by other people. *You* are told about *us* by other people. One of the worst things is not to communicate with each other and let other people communicate in between us.

People are writing books about African Americans. People are writing books about Africans. And we all know each other through other people's eyes. That's *not the way to go.* And there's a lot of profit made by that. So other people aren't gonna stop doing that.

I think what we should do is what you're doing now. Africans and African Americans should write *their own* books. So we can read about Africans or African Americans through our eyes. And as somebody born and raised *in* the culture, you *really know* what's going on. Not some guy who comes in, hangs out for a couple of weeks at a Holiday Inn "collecting data," trying to legitimize his biases.

So I think what you're doing is the right thing. The public needs to learn about African Americans *through* African Americans. We need to learn about Africans *through* Africans. The opinions found in *our* books, you'll never find anywhere because nobody cared to dig that deep. We talk about *real* African religion. African medicine. Gender issues are dealt with in *Precious Mt. Silinda.* Instead of waiting for other people to write about us, we should write about ourselves.

In the end, who's gonna be believed? Me as an African talking about Africans? Or a foreign person writing about Africans? We've been very passive in terms of writing about ourselves and waiting for someone to write about us. And, obviously, we are not very pleased with most of the things that they express because they are definitely inaccurate.

Alexandria White and Jamal Bey
"The Power Couple"

The number of stay-at-home Dads has doubled in the last 25 years, reaching a peak of 2.2 million in 2010, according to a new report by the Pew Research Center. And although the Great Recession contributed to a sharp uptick, by far, the fastest growing segment of at-home Dads say they're home taking care of the kids because they want to be…but now there's been a great change in society. And there's a great term for a guy who takes care of his kids. It's "Dad."

Statistics by Pew Research Center
From the article
"Don't Call them Mr. Mom"
by Brigid Schulte
www.washingtonpost.com
June 5, 2014

For any man, staying at home while his woman goes out and works, this would be an adjustment that would take some humility. I've had to struggle within myself because there is a certain amount of power that comes along with being the breadwinner, right?

JAMAL BEY

A TRUE "POWER COUPLE," JAMAL Bey and his divine partner, Alexandria (Alex) White, exude confidence, energy, creativity, positivity, love, and strength. They feed off of each other's energy. In short, they are custom made for each other.

Their two-year-old son, Ausar, is a physical manifestation of Jamal and Alex's love, energy, and positivity, as a couple. By virtue of his name, Ausar represents a rebirth, a resurrection, and the power to come back and return to greatness.

It is in this inevitable return to greatness, through a love of and knowledge of self, that Alex and Jamal believe that Black people can collectively become "reborn."

This power couple shares their trials, tribulations, testimonies, and triumphs, as they embrace nontraditional roles. Within this particular couple, the mother, Alex, is thirty-four years old, works as a professor of English, women's and cultural studies. Meanwhile, as the father, thirty-five year old Jamal is a stay-at-home dad who is a day trader. An interesting dynamic indeed.

ALEX: Our son, Ausar, his name is the Egyptian, the Kemetic form of Osiris. So one of the original deities. Osiris is one of those myths based on the resurrection of the divine male spirit. So he represents fertility and rebirth. Osiris comes back in springtime. He comes back.

Isis and Osiris are the Greek forms of the names. The Kemetic terms are Auset, which is Isis, and Ausar, which is Osiris. And so Auset rose Ausar up after Ausar was killed by his brother. His brother killed him and scattered his remains all over Earth. So Auset, Ausar's wife, traveled around putting Ausar's parts back together and resurrected him.

That's really powerful because Ausar gets killed *by his brother*. So that's something that we are trying to transmute as a community.

We have to get beyond these petty divisions that are not allowing us to see the divinity in each other. We have to rise above all that petty stuff. Jealousy, greed, all these lower emotions. Operating on that allows you to kill somebody who looks just like you without even thinking about it. To kill your brother, literally.

ALEX: I probably knew within two or three weeks after I conceived. I could feel it. I'm very in touch with my body. And actually, I was working on a lot of things. I was working on my own development, being more in touch with my womb energy, my womb power, claiming that in a very loving way. I was sort of reconditioning myself.

I know the date that we conceived. I know the date that the egg burrowed into my freakin' uterine lining! I remember that feeling. I was thinking, "Okay." But I still didn't want to believe it. We were at a wedding in Big Sur. I woke up before dawn. Ausar was talking to me. He was like, "Mommy, I'm here." So I woke up *freaking out*. Jamal asked me what was wrong. A couple days later, we took a test and confirmed it.

JAMAL: I felt happy. As a matter of fact, I was very happy. At first, I didn't really know what to feel. It was such a shock. It took me a minute to digest it all. Took me a couple of days.

Ausar even arriving didn't even digest until days after he was born and here. But I felt extremely happy, and right away my mind started goin' fast forward. I started puttin' these things in mind as to what needed to be done.

I started thinking about the action, the legwork that was gonna need to take place over the course of the next couple of years as we go into this time of transition. But it was an exciting time.

ALEX: We got our auras read, and this psychic woman said that Jamal had a baby bean in his auric field. There's a spirit in his auric field trying to get through.

JAMAL: And so I asked her, "What's a baby bean?" She said, "Well, you have a spirit that wants to come through." And so…

ALEX: It was all destiny, in my opinion. Really thinking back on it, it was *all destiny.* It was all meant to happen the way it's supposed to happen. Firstly, how I reacted to the pregnancy. I was really scared. I didn't know what to expect. I was just goin' off him, off his energy. Because, obviously, I believe that we, as women, have a choice because *we* have to carry. We're the vessel. So we have a choice in terms of what we wanna do with our bodies.

And I always knew that I wasn't interested in being a single mother, right? He and I weren't married. We had our own studios. We loved our lives, separate lives, but we also loved the time we spent together. We enjoyed each other's time. But it was never like, "Oh, we're gonna have kids next year."

So I was really like, "Do you know what you wanna do? 'Cause if you don't want this baby, if you're feeling insecure at all about your role as a father, then I'll do what I have to do. 'Cause I'm not about to do this by myself."

I had a father in my life. I know the importance of a stable family. I know that's a really important thing for our communities, having that stability. And not to say there's anything wrong with being a single mother. It's just that I know I have the choice as a woman, and I embrace that choice fully.

When I saw Jamal was excited and genuinely happy and said, "Baby, let's do this," then I was like, "All right, let's do this shit." 'Cause there's no guarantees anyway. There's no guarantees that your partner's gonna be there even *if you do* get married.

But now I realize that it was a community involved, there's a village here. It's not *just* Jamal and I that raise this baby. My mom plays a big role in this. My sister, my friends. We have a lot of help with him, and he gets a lot of exposure to different types of people who are family. So I'm not worried. I know that if anything happened to my divine partner that I'll be taken care of, and we will be taken care of.

Jamal's mom's gonna move in with us soon. She's out in Atlanta by herself. What is she out there by herself for? Her only grandchild is here.

So she'll be here in a couple of months with us. And my mother lives not very far away. My sister lives five minutes away. Eventually, we're all gonna try to put our resources, all our money together and get a nice fat spot so we can just really have a clan. We're on that clan vibe right now.

JAMAL: I had already made the commitment that, regardless of the situation, I would never leave my child or anything like that. My real father got locked up when I was two years old. So I didn't really ever have that. I have one memory of my dad all my life until I was about twenty-four.

I worked for an attorney who did collections. He had this system where you could pretty much find anybody. I just typed in his name one day. Boom! All this stuff popped up. I said, "I'm gonna give this guy a call." And that's how we actually got contacted.

Not having him there. *And* he got locked up. I always had this negative idea about my father, in regards to him being arrested, him being locked up and not being in my life because he was messin' around. So from a young age I always felt like *I* was never gonna make those mistakes, you know?

ALEX: So it was an adjustment. It was an adjustment because all of a sudden, with me and Jamal, our relationship became much more serious. It went from being this fun-loving thing to being something much more serious. And he handled it.

He moved in here. We decided to get a midwife. Decided that we were gonna have a home birth. Then I decided that I wanted to be surprised with the gender. I just wanted to be surprised. And I had dreams about a male child. Then other people were having dreams. So even before he was here, we knew he was a boy. Even my father was like, "I got a grandson coming!"

So many of our kids have been taken out, and so many of the Freedom Fighters. So many of the male vibes. It's like they're coming back now! These souls are *coming back*. I know that reincarnation exists. There's no doubt in my mind.

JAMAL: My mom remarried when I was six to a man named Bobby. And really interesting, I'm from Boston originally. Boston has some interesting race relations. A community and city that's majority Irish and Italian. So the Black population is really segregated to a small area of the city. So somehow mom met a man from Southie. It's the very Irish part of town.

So Bobby raised me from the time where I was pretty much five, six years old until he passed in 2011. He had a love for myself and for my mom that was just really deep. It was really deep in the midst of that racial climate. So I did have that father figure. And I think for me that was so important. It was so imperative. Once I got to a certain age, seventeen, eighteen, I got into this real rebellious stage. He could no longer really hold me or reach me. I had gotten to the point where I was gonna do my own thing.

But it was through his wisdom and his abilities. He was a "man's man" in every sense of the word. Never complained. A very, very quiet guy. He would say a lot in one sentence. He wasn't an emotional guy. He very rarely would give you a hug and say, "I love you." But he was a man of action. He didn't talk much. But at the end of the day, he worked from six in the morning till seven at night *every day,* even Saturdays.

And he took care of my mom. My mom was the epitome of the "angry Black woman" in her prime. Now that she's a grandmother, she's super chill. But back then, my mom was a firecracker. Bobby was able to deal with her with his calm demeanor. I learned a lot from that. I learned a lot from him taking action.

I look to that today, that example. He passed in 2011 from a heart attack coming home from work at seven o'clock at night, after working a twelve-hour shift. He died in my mama's driveway. But to me that was integral, having that man figure. And now me having Ausar, having my son, I really do get more of an appreciation. I got more of an appreciation for the work of single mothers, especially those with boys. 'Cause these boys—man, he's a handful. And he needs a firm hand.

ALEX: Ausar doesn't respond to me in the same way. He just doesn't. I can't use force to get him to do what I want. I have to talk to him. I have to nurture him and love him. But with Jamal, it's just much easier. He can just kind of project this certain voice and demeanor, and Ausar responds much more efficiently.

JAMAL: And I've taken a cue from my pops on that. Because my pops never said a lot to me. Like, for real, when he would say something, I would listen because he wasn't really in the mood to talk a lot. And I've kind of taken that approach to my own son. And it's been working for the most part. He's a typical two-year-old, but he's great. We have a good time.

ALEX: My father comes from a big family. A big, loving family. His mom, his parents were together for sixty years. And they had a lot of children. And they had a lot of love. They all sort of was like a tribe. They all took care of each other, and that was the expectation. So he always had that same loving vibe with our immediate family.

My mom and dad were together for twenty years. They're good friends. They're not together now. They split up when I was nineteen, but they're still really good friends. They had two children together. He adopted my brother 'cause my mom had a son from another man. My brother died when I was six. But my father adopted Chad and loved him like his own.

And he's always been a loving man. My father says, "I love you." He's a seriously sensitive man. He's in touch with his feelings. He's not perfect. But he's always shown his protection through love. He never tried to chase boys away. Never. That wasn't his strategy. He made friends with all my boyfriends. He wanted to see what's in their minds.

My mom was always afraid I'm gonna fuck my life up! By my dad had faith that I knew what I was doing. He had two girls. He raised me to be athletic. He raised me to be assertive. He raised me to be confident. So he raised me with a lot of masculine qualities. I think we need to get away from with these *traditional* roles of just raising women to be demure, docile, weak, always looking to and for male approval.

What if all the men around you are losers? You're looking to get approved by *them*? No, that's not how it needs to go down. I guess my point is Black women need to love ourselves a lot more, and our men will recognize that. And either they'll rise to the occasion, or they will perish. Honestly. We don't need 'em. We really don't need them if they can't see our value, the value in *us*.

The institution of marriage in the European sense, it's designed for a specific type of people. We have to make these institutions work for *us*. That's not indigenous. I consider myself indigenous. That's not indigenous to Africa. It's not natural to African people. It's not natural to people who are indigenous. That's why when you got your mama livin' with you, your grandma livin' with you, it's okay. *That's normal*.

JAMAL: I've noticed that it's okay for other races—Mexicans, Asians, whatever the case may be. It's okay for them to live with, to have three or four generations under one roof. They're not called lazy or they're not looked at by their own people as, "Aw, you livin' with *your mama*." How many times have you heard that as men? You live with your mama for nine months in your mama's body. So we lost some of that in the quest to be Eurocentric as possible.

ALEX: And that starts at home. I was saying, we have to teach our kids how to love. That's the conditioning we *have to have.* We have to teach boys to respect their mother. That's so important. So that's what I'm workin' on with my son. He has to respect me immensely because I'm the first woman that he encounters. I set the tone for how he treats every other woman.

So none of this spoiling boys and giving them special privileges. None of these double standards. None of this, "You just like your daddy." No. It's all love. That's the only option we have right now, in my opinion. That and claiming the ancient wisdom of our ancestors. Thought and civilization.

I just know that I've been preparing myself for this moment my whole life. Conditioning myself. Doing the right things. Running, eating right, being positive, doing and just being a loving person. It's not easy to transmute all that negative shit that's comin' at us every day. Nobody is gonna save *us.* We have to save ourselves.

Obama has given us a lot of hope, symbolically. He's just a figure-head. He can't really do anything. But I think he's given a lot of Black people hope on a symbolic level. We have a lot of amazing history and leaders. There's a lot of beauty to be explored in our culture. I feel like the power system is getting scared. That's why they keep trying to show us that they can take us out. I think that's a fear tactic, honestly.

We're a loving people. We've done so much and given so much to this culture, this larger culture. We've given to world culture. So I know that our purpose as souls on this planet is to ignore all that negative stuff that's out there. To transmute all of that negative energy that they're putting at us. They're killing our kids every day. But you can't stop us. They can kill whoever. We're rising. We're changing. We're improving. We're gonna get our stuff together. That's what they're scared of. That's why they're killing these little Black kids. How does a grown man get scared of a sixteen-year-old Black kid?

JAMAL: We have to understand that the directive was put out back even before the sixties with J. Edgar Hoover. We must at all cost stop the rise of the Black messiah. Stop the unification of the Black military groups, these militant groups. So when you look at the role that the media has played from that perspective, it's very obvious. From the music we listen to, from the news images, from everything else, their only job is to prevent that from happening. I feel like these shows that we watch, Empire, Atlanta Housewives, and all that. It keeps us at a certain vibration that is just dealing in our lower nature. Lower emotions.

I think it's important for us to see the signs and symbols. Not just look at things literally. But look at the messages that they're sending us. Why do they keep inundating us with slave movies?

Now some will look and say, "Wait a minute. Those are innocent movies. They educate me. I get to see a little bit of my history and what our people did." But that's not our *true history*. That is a road bump. A speed bump in a long highway of our information. It's a moment in our history. But it's a moment in our history that puts us in a position of subservience, always.

ALEX: We are not slaves. You're a slave if you believe you're a slave. Not all slaves believed they were slaves. This is the mental challenge. Why did Harriet Tubman *not* believe it? Why did Nat Turner *not* believe it? Why did Frederick Douglass *not* believe it? It's powerful. My point is that not everything, all the stories and ideologies that have been put into us and supported by the European is actual and factual. We accept it all the time. Just like we accept Jesus Christ as being European and never ask about the truth.

ALEX: I've been thinkin' about this a lot. I've even thought about starting a parenting blog about how to get and give some strategies on how to raise a strong, fulfilled Black young person in this world today. Like, create our *own* culture in our *own* space based on what *we* need. And I think we can take the wisdom of all cultures. Because I think that every culture has something to offer.

We create our own space, our own culture in here. Ausar, Jamal, Alex. Our space is buffered. We keep a bubble. I don't let fear into here, for one. There's *no* Call of Duty, Atlanta Housewives. No violence on my TV. None of that crazy shit is allowed in here. The stuff that maybe others would see as normal.

I think another thing we have to do is question what is *considered normal*. We need to question everything. I've done that my whole life. So that's why I feel like I'm at this place where I am now. The media's a big thing. Just being more aware of what Ausar's being exposed to and the people he's being exposed to as well.

I've been thinking about how to teach him to be a more compassionate person. And I think compassion has to go hand in hand with intellect. We want all of our babies to be smart. But we also need our babies to be good people. I think a lot of the problem with our community is just we don't know how to treat each other. We just don't. That's part of our being colonized. To divide and conquer. So I just wanna teach him those values like compassion, integrity, love. He'll know how to conduct himself when he gets in awkward situations. He'll know how to conduct himself when he deals with authority. He'll stand up for himself and know he's really free.

JAMAL: I think having a thorough knowledge of self, you know who you are, know who you come from. You know that your history does not begin in subjection. You know your history begins in glory and greatness. That will help to ease some of the self-hate that we seem to be almost born with. But a lot of that is from not only the imagery we're exposed to but the conditioning of our parents.

ALEX: Every human being's first home is their mother's womb. That's the first territory we all occupy. For women, we have to love ourselves. 'Cause if we're sending real hate, hateful anger, rage, resentment, shame, and guilt, our wombs are toxic. They're supposed to be incubators of love. That's why I'm sayin' we have to transmute all that negative shit.

It's not natural to kill your children. But that's what some slave women would do. They would kill their own babies. What we see now with all that Black-on-Black killing. That's psychopathic. That's sociopathic. It's a mental illness. It's a pathology.

It's not just Black people goin' crazy. What kind of craziness does it take for you to feel justified in killing a seventeen-year-old boy and you think that it's okay? These White folks are goin' crazy too! It's happening in both directions. We can't control everybody else's emotions, but we can control ours. It's a war on our babies. And the war is happening in an invisible space. It's happening in the realm of thought firstly. The realm of thought emotion. These negative energies make people devilish. Fear and hate is the root cause of evil.

JAMAL: This is a secret weapon for silent wars. The weapons that they are using are so subvert and so psychological that it's very, very hard for someone to even understand the weaponry being used upon them.

JAMAL: It was a very organic type of decision for me to be a stay-at-home dad. Organic in the sense that it wasn't something that we really needed to debate or really kind of discuss in a long-term type of sense. It really arose out of the natural way that our situation was progressing and our ability to accept things as they are. To be adaptable to our situation.

In *The Parable of the Sower,* Octavia Butler says in her book, "God is change." So we have to shape it the way that works for us. Because shapes change. The way our situation kinda transitioned, I was transitioning into different careers. I had a video-production company, and I was doing real estate at the time. Things just fizzled out, though.

I sold my first property, and so that was perfect timing. So we just chilled for a minute.

ALEX: I only worked for one trimester of my pregnancy. I worked a little bit in my second trimester. And then I had my last trimester off. Then I had the first nine months home with Ausar. And a lotta women don't get that. I didn't even leave the house for the first six weeks after I gave birth.

I gave birth in my house. In my room. I didn't have to leave the house for six weeks. People—everyone—took care of me. Jamal took care of me. My mom took care of me. My sister, my friends. So I was nurtured. And that was an interesting experience in itself. I'm used to being very active, used to being on the go, being free and doing my own thing.

JAMAL: And it was an interesting time for me because I was gone a lot of the time. At that time our roles were reversed. I was traveling a lot for work. I'd be gone all day. But at the end of the day, we had what we needed. We had more than what we needed. And I think at this point, we've both accepted that we have to work together, whatever that involves. It's really about what's best for Ausar.

Again, I make this correlation, you look at other races. The men, they'll work things out, right? The men will go back to school while the wife works. Then, when the man gets his degree, he'll work, and his wife will focus on her small business or on her going back to school. And when that gets off the ground, they'll alternate back and forth.

ALEX: For us too, as women, we're always looking at what a man has. We don't see him for *who he is*. What kind of car he has. How much money or the shoes he's wearing. And men do it too. It's an illusion. It's a façade. And it's a distraction.

So I recognized at a young age that I don't care about what people have. I care more about who they are. Everyone's divine because they're alive. But for me—for us—I think it got to a point where I was able to be like, "I gotta do what I gotta do right now." Just take care of my family.

It's a struggle. It's not easy. It's been an adjustment. It's an adjustment to these new gender roles. And I'll just say that I have gained a new appreciation for what it means to be a *breadwinner.* The pressure that is placed on men to be that. I've gained a new appreciation for men. Just like Jamal's gained a new appreciation for what it takes to "run a house."

I think it's important we are experiencing these differences. Now I know why some men resent having to make the money. Now I can see how they might feel when they come home and expect certain things from women. And I think Jamal can now see why women "go crazy" in the house all day. It's challenging to actually manage and maintain a household. It's not easy to maintain the house.

Women get stuck in the house so the man can go out and be the breadwinner. This is a women's rights issue. This is *unpaid labor.* Capitalism is always lookin' for a way not to pay people. Whether it's the migrant worker, whether it's the woman, it's the slave, whatever. It's a way to control a woman's power. You marry a woman, she takes care of you, you get free labor outta her, and you can basically go out and do your thing. That's a Eurocentric perspective of it. So for me to go out and work and for Jamal to stay at home, we embody the principles that work for *us.* I don't give a shit about those gender roles. Those are just roles. That doesn't mean anything to me. I'm doing what I have to do to take care of my family. I'm happy too. I haven't been this happy in my whole life. I'm very happy right now 'cause I'm livin' freely. I'm not living according to roles.

Of course my mom comes here like, "Oh, he needs to go do this. Oh, he needs to go do that. Why isn't he doing this?" Somebody's always gonna tell you what you need to do with *your* life. *We* have to be strong and decide what's best for *us.* Right now, Jamal is taking time to develop himself in his field as a trader. So he needs to be here.

He's working on himself and his craft. And as long as I see that, I'm always gonna support him.

JAMAL For any man, staying at home while his woman goes out and works, this would be an adjustment that would take some humility. I've had to struggle within myself because there is a certain amount of power that comes along with being the breadwinner, right? There's meaning. Like, "I got the money, so I call the shots." It's an illusion of power. And it's very easy for us, as men, to feel like, "Okay, I own *all this*. All this is *mine*."

So to step down from that. To come down from that for a second is very humbling. It's a very humbling experience. And it's not easy in the state of mind we have as men. I have men all the time say to me, "Man, most guys just wouldn't do what you do, man." Like, "I listen to y'all, I look at y'all man, you and your son and…I couldn't do it."

So I see it, I understand that it's not a usual thing. I mean, it's to the point where if I'm walking with Ausar, I've had cops pull up to me, while walking with him, tell me "That's what we like to see." It kind of upset me, truth be told. I just looked at him. It was a backhanded compliment. It didn't make me feel good. I didn't even respond. He was showin' how most people look at us. And how they blame us for our own problems.

ALEX: They think it's okay to kill a Black baby 'cause he ain't got a daddy. Does that make it okay to kill a Black person? Just 'cause he ain't got a daddy? That don't make no damn sense. Our culture is crazy.

JAMAL: And it's a proverbial "Daddy", in some cases. It ain't just a real, literal daddy. It's the proverbial *daddy of your people* that needs to be policed. Your people need to be *fathered*. Because you don't have no daddy. It's threatening.

And so I get that from brothers all the time too. Ausar and I took the bus. And several times they've just let me on the bus for free. Like, "Go ahead." I get it all the time, and it's cool. But it makes me hypersensitive to the father/son relationships. Now when I see a dad, I give him the nod. I'm like, "Yup." 'Cause we're like considered an anomaly. But in reality, Black dads are not an anomaly. We're not.

JAMAL: My advice to couples in balancing life, work, and trying to co-parent is to bring the family together. It's not supposed to be done with just two people. It's so hard that you almost can't. Unless one person is making over six figures. In California, you got to be making at least a hundred twenty grand. One fifty to be comfortable. We're not there. So we need family. Family support.

ALEX: We have a working class, middle class income. So we have to bring family in. We're strategizing on how to bring more wealth into our home. We bring more people in. And they share. Many hands make light work. But that means we have to all work together. We gotta learn to work together.

Even with other African groups, they bring over the grandmother, the grandfather, two, three generations in the same house. Accumulate that wealth. Buy the house, then buy the house next to it. That's our plan. 'Cause we love each other. We don't have a dysfunctional relationship. Love is energy. We need love to transform. Money's energy too. Money's currency. We gotta transform that love into currency, transform it into real estate, into a legacy for Ausar.

ALEX: Jamal, he's like a lion. A calm lion. A lion comes to mind because it's just like the Rastas say: it's a powerful figure. A power symbol. He doesn't have to do much. It's just his presence that sets the tone. That daddy presence, right? His presence. His demeanor. He's always been cool and calm and confident. He never gets worked up. He's more patient than I am. He just knows how to deal with Ausar in a better way than I. Sometimes I get too frustrated. But he's just very calm but strong and is able to handle it. He handles it.

JAMAL: I marvel at Alex's abilities, her compassion and her love. And her ability to convey that just in little hugs. Very, very thoughtful. And I'm grateful that Ausar's gonna have that because men need that. Black men need thoughtfulness, especially as it pertains to Black women. It's a work in progress for me to become more mindful of being thoughtful. Being the thinking heart.

I think she's a great teacher. The first teacher. She's the source of all of his emotion. When Ausar's upset, it's mommy. When he's happy, it's mommy. When she comes home, it's mommy. You know a lot of his emotion is driven through his mother. And her ability to absorb emotion and give it back is remarkable. I'm grateful he has that. That he can learn two sides and not be rigid. He's gonna have a sensitive side too. A range of emotion. He gets that from her.

JAMAL: [I plan on]Teaching him about Kemetic history. Teaching him about the Moors as they traveled the world and engaged with different European cultures. I gotta teach him all of that alternative history, ancient history. But then bring it forward to what is the practical solution for right now? In our choices that we've made with his future, everything we've done is to set him up to be successful.

ALEX: We have to not just teach culture but just teach him how to love the little things. Like, love *everything*. Appreciate it all. Focusing on gratitude and appreciation and love. And not teaching fear. That's what I'm focusing on.

It's been weird for me 'cause I've been, we've been conditioned. As a woman, you're conditioned to be the *nurturer*. We're conditioned to stay at home and be passive. And the opposite is true for the man. So I'm learning more about my abilities, my capacity to be a more complete human being. More of what I'm capable of as a woman. I can be a nurturer *and* a provider. And those two things can coexist. And so can Jamal. Superseding these roles is the only way we're gonna get out of this quagmire we're in. If we internalize all these things we're being told, we will go crazy.

JAMAL: I'm about to go scrub him up. I actually thought about a memory that I had of my dad when I was two years old. My biological dad when I was two years old. That's the *only* memory I had of him. And I thought to myself, "Ausar will remember this moment." He will remember daddy scrubbin' him up in the bathtub. Daddy changin' his diapers. Daddy pickin' him up. He's gonna remember that, and those experiences are forming the bond that we're gonna have forever. And I really had to appreciate that because I only have one memory of my real dad. Ausar, he's gonna have millions of 'em.

Stanley Cox AKA Mistah F.A.B.
"From Dope Era to Daddy"

*By definition co-parenting is a parenting situation
where the parents are not in a marriage, cohabitation
or romantic relationship with one another, they are
simply providing a two-parent system for a child.*

*From the article
"Black Co-Parenting"
by Krystal Glass
May, 2013*

I wanna be the first man that she loves. Her first love.
And those are things that you just gotta try. And it's
hard to do those things when you didn't have a father.
So it becomes a trial and error, but you can't make that
excuse. Because when you make that excuse, that means you're
setting yourself up to repeat the same mistakes
that previously happened to you.

STANLEY COX AKA MISTAH F.A.B.

THERE'S NO WAY TO DENY the worldwide influence of hip-hop music and culture. It's hard to imagine that this "rebellious" music, art form, and culture is now given mainstream credit and credence. Who, in 1979 in the Bronx, New York, could fathom that the music containing the poverty, despair, and socio-economic struggles of Black and Latino youth would transcend language, cultures, time and boundaries?

Hip-hop music and culture is a powerful medium of self-expression. Artists like Dr. Dre, Jay-Z, Nas, 50 Cent, and Lil Wayne have each become household names. They've been embraced by Middle America and corporate America alike. Even though hip-hop music and its artists are often blanketed with terms like "misogynistic," "homophobic," or "violent," hip-hop continues to be the voice of the young generation.

Getting to speak candidly with hip-hop artist Mistah F.A.B. was enlightening and eye-opening. We often think we know artists through their social-media posts, music videos, or radio songs. However, we hardly get a glimpse into their day-to-day lives.

Mistah F.A.B. opened up regarding his life, his influences, and the love he has for his mother and daughter. Not to mention, he revealed a side that most people may not see. He spoke to me as Stanley Cox, the father, the community organizer, and the philanthropist. Fortunately Stanley didn't allow Mistah F.A.B., the artist, to take center stage in this interview. On top of that, he and I conducted our interview and discussion outside. We sat on a busy corner of the Oakland, California, neighborhood where he grew up.

STANLEY: I'm Stanley Cox, aka Mistah F.A.B. My occupation is independent business owner, entrepreneur, hustler, philanthropist, many different things that go around the name of occupation. *Survivor* is what I like to put out there the most. My beautiful daughter, Liberty. Liberty Forever Free Cox. That's my daughter, and she's seven years old. She's a second grader. And she's my *everything*.

One of the reasons why I wanted to do this interview right here (outside on the corner) particularly is this is where I'm from. This is what we considered the dope era. Where I grew up at, right here on this corner, I watched several of my friends lose their lives— whether it was physically losing their life or throwin' their life away by the things they were involved in. I'm not tryin' to popularize it, but right here on this same corner, I seen a lot of people give up on life. Whether they were sellin' drugs, usin' drugs, and that was the dope era. That was the thing I grew up in. That was what I watched when I walked to the store. A casual walk to the store could mean anything. It could mean you seein' somebody get a lotta money. It could mean you seein' whatever. Just one trip to the store could mean a lot.

So with the Dope Era clothing line, it's something I felt like, through fashion, I wanna rekindle some of those memories, whether they be good or bad. But I also wanted to give you a perspective on what I was goin' through. So some of the things that was humiliating, and some of the things that were the experiences, the trials and tribulations we went through in this era actually made us our most creative. So through fashion we are able to relive those moments. Dope Era is an acronym that stands for During Oppression People Evolve Everyone Rises Above.

We do a lot with videogames in our clothing. Those were happy moments. Those are things that everyone can relate to as kids from the eighties and early nineties. With each one of our threads, our pieces, it's something that takes you back where you be like. "Yo, I remember that!" And I think that alone makes it bigger than just clothing. You bring in generations.

You got the older generation, who when the younger generation sees it and don't understand it, they be like, "You know how old I was when I had that? When that came out..." So we're meshing and blending generations. And it's like the dope era. You gotta come see me. You gotta meet up with me, and you can get it right out the trunk, man. We serve it right out the trunk.

Everything to me is significant to this corner. From charity events to block parties to setting up pop-up shops, right here on this corner. Forty-fifth and Market, man. I got so much from this corner. I got so much from this neighborhood. I learned so much. I experienced so much. But with our charity events, we come right back here to this same corner. Or we take it to the basketball court where I grew up at down the street. Before it was rap, it was sports. Like anywhere in the inner-city community, you got three-pointers or street corners.

Once I was able to be in a position to utilize my influence for the greater good, I wanted to do so. If I was able to be in position financially, I would utilize that to galvanize many others who are in position to help those without. To organize a group of haves to help those who have not. And that's what we do, man.

So for the past eight, nine years, every year, all throughout the year, we do community events. And to me, that's far more important than anything that I've done musically. It goes longer, and those memories never fade. A person will forget a song lyric. But they'll never forget you feedin' their families. Or never forget you givin' their children some gifts during Christmas when they were goin' through some hard times. Those things are priceless.

The significance of the male figure in the community events is pretty relevant. We employ a lot of people. We have some of the neighborhood guys, who certain people judge and look down upon, the castaways, aka the drug addicts or whatever. Whatever people look at them as. You know, to me, they're my unc or the big homies. But we employ those dudes. So whether it be cleanin' up, whether it be cookin', grillin', helpin' piece the stuff together, we employ those dudes. We give out opportunity. I don't judge nobody.

And I would love to see more Blacks even bein' more significantly involved by doin' these things in their communities. I would love to see that. I would love to see some of my brothers who have, do certain things. Whether if it's on a smaller scale or, hopefully, on a broader scale. The main purpose of it is let's just *do it.* Let's utilize our influence to help out, man. You never know what we could do.

My mama was my biggest male influence. My mom played *all roles.* She was a very strong individual. My dad passed away when I was twelve. Good dude, though. Take nothin' away from him. Loving dude. But outside of my mother, a lot of the athletes influenced me and some of the big homies here.

One person that always sticks out in my mind though is Donyell Marshall. He used to play for the Golden State Warriors. He was comin' outta UConn. He had signed with the Warriors after comin' from Minnesota. My mom was heavy into the promotin' and club scenes. She would have these events where a lotta the athletes would come out.

And she hooked up with Donyell one day and was telling him how she was a single mother. How hard it was raisin' a teenager. He said he had a brother my age that comes to stay with him during the summers. So when his brother got out here, he would come get me, and we could all just go hoop and play basketball. And he stuck to his word, bro. I remember bein' like thirteen, fourteen years old, man. And for the first time, he came and got me. I was just shocked like, "Damn, this is *Donyell Marshall*."

I just seen this dude on TV! This is the Big Ten Player of the Year. You feel me? When he was playin' at UConn, I had just watched him in the Final Four. And I think that year he signed one of them *big* contracts. So he was havin' some money. We would go up to the house, up in the hills. A super-huge house, the cars, the Benzes, the Lexuses. He had the arcade games. I was a kid, man. But every summer after that, he would come get me. And that meant a lot to me, bro. *A lot.*

That was the first person outside of my immediate family who actually showed they cared. And it showed me if I ever get in a position like that, I'm gonna take some young dudes under my wing. So Donyell Marshall will *always* be significant in my life for doin' that. It was a lifetime memory that I'll never forget.

But other than that, moms was cold. You feel me? Moms was a hustler. Moms was a gangsta. A mother. Moms was a teacher. Moms was a student. Moms wore a lotta hats, man. And she was everybody's mom in this neighborhood. So she taught me a lot. She couldn't teach me how to be a man. I had to learn that on my own. But she taught me the qualities that men carry. And, you know, not to be no bitch—excuse my language. Don't be a woman. Man up.

I remember when the earthquake hit in '89. I was seein' her gettin' stuff together, grabbin' stuff. I was like, "Mom, what you doin'?" She was like, "Man, I'm gonna go help these people that's trapped on the freeway. Baby, there's some people trapped on the freeway that collapsed. They need our help. As a community, they need our help. We all gotta play a role."

I was too young to really understand that. But I remember it. She was always willin' to be on the front line to go help somebody. To give people opportunity. I seen a lotta that at a young age. And it was like, "Damn. Moms is like Superwoman." She taught me how to love.

Taught me how to care about somebody. So I'm just comin' full circle in doin' my own community thing. It's beautiful.

[Men need to possess] Honesty and loyalty, man. Sometimes we wanna judge people who don't have a relationship with their father. You don't know what was goin' on in your father's life at that time. You don't know these things that went on between him and your mother. You gotta give a person a chance.

But at the end of the day, as men, we gotta want that chance. You gotta take advantage of that chance. Take those opportunities. You know, my biggest fear is somebody else tellin' my daughter how I was. So I'd rather be there so I can experience that. I wanna be able to experience life with my daughter. To be there with my daughter. I wanna be able to teach her the things that my dad wanted to explain to me but I was too young to understand those jewels. I wanna be the positive influence that I saw in some of my friends' fathers. And set the bar, set the example.

I wanna be the first man that she loves. Her *first love*. And those are things that you just gotta try. And it's hard to do those things when you didn't have a father. So it becomes a trial and error. But you can't make that excuse. Because when you make that excuse, that means you're setting yourself up to repeat the same mistakes that previously happened to you.

And with my daughter, I let her know that daddy has a job, a career. Whether she fully understands it, she knows that part of daddy's job is goin' out doin' what he has to do to come back home to be able to provide. I have a seven-year-old, but she's far more advanced than that. So her ability to grasp certain things and understand certain things.

She's on it. She's like, "So when you get back, since you out on the road workin', I need this, and I want this." She's workin' her bargaining game already. Workin' her barter system. She's a cold piece, man. But you have to *wanna do it*. You have to wanna be a father, man. You have to be able to be in your child's life. 'Cause if you not....

When I found out I was gonna have a girl, I was like, "Whoa. Whoa, this is crazy!" But we planned it. When we were younger, we had a run where it didn't go so well. I told her—her being my daughter's mother—I was like, "Yo, I'm gonna give you a baby. I owe you that. I owe you for all the stuff that I put you through." We've been talkin' for years, man. And when we found out, it was like, "Yeah. That's what's up." And it really changed me, man. It changed me damn near instantly.

I was like, "Well, I'm gonna stop smokin' weed. Stop sippin syrup. Stop drinking alcohol. Stop doing all that stuff." And, I did it, you know. It was time to just...you wanna be the influence that you want your child to see. People tend to forget that when your kid grow up seein' that type of stuff, in their mind, they think, "Okay, my parents do it, so it's not wrong. My parents doin' it. So I wanna do that." Your parents. That's the first influence.

So I could say in seven years of my daughter's life, she's never seen me drink. Never seen me smoke. Never seen me do none of that. And I stuck to my word. I haven't drank or smoked in damn near seven years. And she can count on her hands how many times she probably even heard me cuss around her. Like I said, I wanna be the first positive influence on her life. I continue to let her know what it's about. I'm not a perfect person, but I'm tryin' and growin', and she sees that.

Yeah, it's a very *conscious* decision. You gotta be stern, man. You gotta stand on what you believe in. Stand on your principles. It's easy to get caught up and fall victim under the influence of what everybody else is doin'. So you gotta be a strong individual. Gotta stay on concrete ground. Doin' wrong is *easy*, bro. Like they say, it's easy to kill a person. It's harder to let someone live. Especially when you in that field and you're in survival mode.

So you gotta stand on what you believe in. Even if you're the only one standin'. And I just stick to my guns. I've been around 'em all. I'll be around Snoop, and Snoop be like, "Man, hit the weed." I tell him, "I don't smoke." I mean, you know how many people would jump at the opportunity to smoke with Snoop? But I'm like, "I'm cool, big bro. That ain't my thing." And when people see that you solid to your morals, then they ease off. People will always try to test you. Of course, you gotta deal with, "Ahhh, man, you're a square." Ain't nothin' wrong with bein' a square. Squares live longer, man.

Co-parenting is pivotal in the success of the development of your child, mentally, spiritually, and greater safety of them physically. It's a great thing to do, whether you see eye-to-eye with your partner. Y'all don't have to be together. But it's something that you have to do. It's the mature thing.

One of the rude awakenings is when I seen my daughter's mom post a picture of her and her boyfriend. That was like, "Whoa." Like, "What? Hold on! Wait. I wasn't ready!" Like, "Wait a minute. What's this?" This is somebody who I've been dealing with and involved with since eleventh, twelfth grade. And that was the first man I ever seen that *wasn't me* with her. You ever be so mad that you don't say *nothin'*?

But what that spawned is the growth of my understanding that, as a woman, she has to move forward with her life as well. She just can't wait for me to finally be in a relationship or finally give her the attention that she deserves. Or finally treat her as the woman that she longs to be.

And the maturing of that has allowed for our friendship to grow astounding. We've established a grounds as individuals. We don't have to be involved in each other's lives sexually, or relationship-wise, for this to work. But I have to respect you as an individual. And in return, you respect me as an individual. And co-parenting, to be good friends or great parents, is a situation that helps the development of successful possibilities for your child. And it's healthy.

If you're anything like me, you've realized that over the course of the years, you've put your partner through their fair share of rude awakenings. Especially me, being in the public eye. And there comes a time in a man's life where he *has to* grow up. Where he has to say, "Man, I'm not gonna keep toying with you. Keep toying with your heart. Only wantin' you when I want you. Let me let you grow. Let me let you do you." 'Cause when I give up that, it's gonna help me as well.

That emotional attachment, nine outta ten times, it's jealousy. And it's the male being territorial about what he feels belongs to him. And that's not it, bro. That's a woman. That's your child's mother. Allow her to make space and grow for the same respect you would want to. What's good for you *can't* be bad for her. But it takes a lotta maturity. A lot.

[Accountability for your lyrical content] As an artist, it's a big responsibility, man. You have to understand that you're spewing things to these children. That some of them don't understand if it's entertainment or if it's to be taken literally. To some, it's just entertainment. But I think it's a thin line between "You do have an obligation" and "It's just my career."

As an artist, you have to make that keepsake with yourself like, "Man, would I want *my child* listening to this? Would I want *my kid* to be influenced by this? If so do I change up my lyrics a little bit? Do I do somethin' different?"

And as a parent, and as someone who's conscious, you have to be able to say, "Well, where are the parents?" Don't just put all the blame on me! 'Cause I've been blamed for certain things. And I say, "Where are the parents? Apparently, you not bein' the parent."

So to a certain extent, there's an obligation of leadership for artists. Sometimes that leadership may not be through music. It may be through our actions outside of the studio. But I think at one point in every artist's career, when they realize they've reached a level of influence, they should utilize that to help those who don't understand the difference between entertainment and reality.

When I see the Jay-Zs some of those other guys, what I see is someone who came from the same places that I come from. Someone who made it to a level on the magazine cover with Warren Buffett. That's amazing. Like, "Dude, you come from the projects. Now you getting accepted by Blue Blood." That's a *big* step. So that's inspiration for me. Me focusing on the successful Black males. I study success. I see those who are successful, and to me, it's motivation. It lets me know that I can be in that exact same position.

Look at my little cousin Marshawn. People say whatever they wanna say about Marshawn Lynch. But he made it to a level, a stature, and he hasn't changed himself one bit. He just wanna play football. You can't buy into the media. The media, its whole existence and invention of the media is to give news, whether it be good or bad news. And most of the time bad news gets the reviews nowadays. We're more prone to violence. We're more prone to negligence. We love the negativity. We're followin' it like robots.

When you look at someone like Marshawn, they don't tell you a child who comes from a single-parent home. Who comes from the pits of poverty. Who comes from the dungeons of negligence. Who was never given an opportunity. They don't tell you of his rise. They don't say, "He went to Cal-Berkeley, and he's an educated, young

Black man. He goes out and gives back to his community that he lost many of his friends in."

Marshawn gives charity events. He donates millions of dollars to the development and reconstructing of young minds in the community he comes from. He does a lot of philanthropy work. They *never* highlight any of that. The media never talks about what he represents and what he embodies as a man. They just say, "Oh, he doesn't wanna talk to the media. He doesn't wanna do this. Doesn't wanna do that."

So it's like, "My love for this sport has to be diminished by me not wantin' the attention of the media? Not wantin' to let you guys inside of my life? I haven't had great luck with the media in my past. Therefore, I choose not to deal with you guys. And now that I choose that, I'm a bad person? Yeah, I have dreads. Yeah, I have gold teeth. Yeah, I have tattoos. Does that make me a *bad person*? If I didn't have all that, would I be a *good person*?"

We have to look at things. I want kids to know that we've been so brainwashed when it comes to the imagery of who we are. Let's not get caught up in the media image. If we judge things for what they *actually are*, not what they appear to be, we could really come to more of an understanding of what the truth is.

People judge Marshawn without even knowin' him. People judge me without even knowin' me. "Oh, you're a rapper? Then you must do…" When we do our charity events, people be like, "What charity is throwin' this?" We're like, "Just the community." They'll be like, "Okay. So with drug money?" I'm like, "Nah, man. We work hard for this. This is what we do." But this is America. The propaganda. The social media. It will paint you to be the villain even after you're known as a good guy.

What I am most proud of my daughter for is *everything*. Everything, man. Her ability to read and write at an advanced level. You know, she's reading at a fifth- or sixth-grade level. She's traveled. She's been around the world. Her sense of fashion. Her sense of understanding. Her personality. Her creativity. Her ability to dictate what it is that she's feeling. To be able to cover her emotion through conversation. I'm proud of her outlook on life. Even at this young age.

As a father, I'm honest with my daughter. I'm givin' her the opportunities to do things that I wasn't able to do as a kid. I've taken my daughter to Paris, to London, the Caribbean. Disneyworld and Disneyland. I was never able to have those opportunities with my parents. For one, my mama wasn't gettin' on a plane that long.

But to be able to say, "Damn, man. All startin' from this corner with a pen and a pad." I never sold crack. Ain't never had to rob or take nothin' from nobody. So all of my dreams and aspirations, I was able to do that. Bein' able to provide for your child and not takin' nothing from nobody, not stealin' from nobody. Man, that's a blessing. And a great feeling.

And her knowin' her father is out workin' hard for it, man. Not only that, but havin' her come get involved with some of the charity events and philanthropy events. Her givin' out turkeys. Her givin' out gifts to the children. For her to understand that, although we do get and we receive, it's always better to give. The charity that one gives to others is the rent that he pays for his space on Earth. And that's a blessing to be able to instill that in my daughter at seven years old.

I'm just Stan. I'm just Stanley. I never let Mistah F.A.B. get bigger than Stanley to me. Mistah F.A.B. is just my career. But in these parts, I'll always be known as Stanley. And that's the gravity for me. The gravity to keep me here. That gravity continues to keep me to be able to walk these corners. To walk these blocks. No security. Don't gotta bunch of goons outside. It's just me. This neighborhood keeps me grounded. They let me know that no matter how big you get, you still from right here. I could never change where I'm from. I can change where I'm goin'. I could change where I end up. But I can never change this corner right here.

At the end of the day, the legacy reads, "He stayed true to who he was." And I think that's what I'm most proud about. I can look in the mirror and still be happy. I'm somebody that just did him. I always did me, bro. I made the music that I wanted to make. I always set the trends. I did it with my own touch. I was always innovative. The creator of wealth. To be able to create something, create an opportunity for yourself. To not be a mainstream artist. To not be an industry, household name. But to still be known in households. I was never a major artist. But everywhere you go, people know me. I'm accepted by major artists, in their circles. I could call the same people that you can call. I can go on the same trips that you see your favorite artist on. I can do all the same things they do, all from right here, man. Damn near fifteen years in the game and I'm *still right here.*

When they go back and they look at the resume, they'll say, "Damn, that boy was workin'. He got projects. He got time in the game. He did it. And at the end of the day, he never changed. It was always him."

Chris and Tiffani Underwood
"Blended Family and Blended Styles"

*Listen, my son, to your father's instruction and
do not forsake your mother's teaching.*

Proverbs 1:8 NIV

As far as in today's world you see a lot of Black men not bein' there for their kids. But the problem is, there's so many that are. But the number that aren't just outshine those that are. So we just get a bad rap. And nobody's perfect. We all fall short. But make that effort to be in your child's life.

CHRIS UNDERWOOD

THE BARBERSHOP AND BEAUTY SALON have long been considered a sanctuary in the African American community. In fact, since Blacks were routinely excluded from patronizing exclusive country clubs, gentlemen's clubs and secret societies, the barbershops and beauty salons have become our own country clubs. The barbershop and beauty salon have evolved from places to get yourself groomed and looking good, into inclusive, safe spaces.

It is in these shops, these safe spaces, where customers can talk business, politics, sports, fashion, style, love, and relationships, as well as keep abreast of the latest cultural happenings. In fact, barbers and beauticians can become our therapists or counselors while we're in their chairs.

Before deciding to shave my head bald, I was a man who went to the barbershop weekly. It became a "necessity" for me to ensure my hair looked good—*especially so* on the weekends. I'm sure that many other Black men and women can attest to this.

For me, having a good barber, a good stylist, was paramount. I was fortunate to have found my barber, Chris Underwood, several years ago. Over the course of those years, I've followed Chris to several different shops that he's operated in. I even went to his house to get cut, when he was in between shops. As my barber, I found Chris to be on time, efficient, professional, stylish, and articulate. But, most importantly, Chris had *skills* with the clipper and straight edge razor.

Chris, and his wife, Tiffani have been a duo in the hair business for many years. In fact, as long as I've known Chris, Tiff has done hair in the same shops as he has. The two own a business and are raising their two kids together. The couple has a "blended family," and they shared their experiences managing relationships, business, and parenting.

CHRIS: My name is Chris Underwood. I am thirty-three years old. I am married to Tiffani Underwood. We've been married for goin' on eight years now. I'm a licensed barber. I've been licensed for thirteen years now. It's my passion. I love doin' it. Father of two kids, Destiny and Christopher, Jr. Christopher is eight, and Destiny is fifteen.

TIFFANI: I'm Tiffani Underwood. I am thirty-three. I'm married to Chris Underwood. Mother of two children. I am a licensed cosmetologist/co-owner of the salon. The shop is Blended Styles.

CHRIS: February 2015 will make one year that we've owned the shop and been in operation here. Newlyweds in the shop sense. In the business owner sense. It feels good. It's a long time comin'.

Here at Blended Styles, my wife, she's really good with talkin' with her clients. She tells her clients exactly what they need for their hair. We're more than *just stylists*. We're therapists too. I have clients that come in and have issues. "What's your opinion on this? What's your opinion on that?"

In the barbershop, the stereotypical setting, you can see a movie where guys are hangin' out. They might be hangin' out front. Or somebody might be playin' checkers. You may have the old heads in the shop playin' chess. Just hangin' out and chillin'. But we have a good sense of our clients and what they need. They come to us with their problems. And with good things too. We always converse with our clients. We have a good rapport with them.

TIFFANI: On the female side, we talk about men, of course. We talk about relationships and family. I don't do gossip at all. Some women are used to comin' to the salon to talk about other women. I usually say, "Well, that's too bad." I just shut it down. And move on. Some women come to talk about church. Just to share events that they might have goin' on at church or at their jobs. So it's definitely networking. I have no problem saying yes or no to a style. I tell them why. So they appreciate that.

My longest client, I've had her since beauty school. I was in beauty when I was sixteen. So she's been my client since I was sixteen. She's followed me everywhere I went.

CHRIS: Yeah, Tiff's been doin' hair longer than I have. And for her to have a client for that long is great. I think the longest client I've had probably is about eight years. Loyal, loyal. That's the livelihood. I don't have *any other* job beside bein' a husband and a father.

CHRIS: Growin' up, I come from a two-parent household. A lot of us can't say that. My father has been there since day one. I got a really strong representation of what fatherhood is about. So I've had key points in my life that my dad has always been there. Sports games. Graduations. Recitals, everything. So I got that fatherhood guideline, that blue-print from my father.

And my grandfather. My grandpa was always there and always around. He picked me up from school sometimes when my parents couldn't come get me. So I've *always had* those two strong, male fig-ures in my life. My grandfather and my father. They've always been there. Strong role models. Very strong.

First and foremost, they're God-fearing. I am a Christian, myself. I think men should, first and foremost, know where everything comes from. God is everything. So without Him, we would have nothing.

So God, truthfulness, honesty, doin' things that you say you're gonna do. We all fall short. Nobody's perfect. But I think those are characteristics that you can look up to. And just being there. Being supportive. Being able to talk to, being able to relate to. Without those characteristics, it's hard to raise a child. If you don't have the basics, it's hard to tell someone else what to do. Those are some key characteristics. And being able to provide too. Of course, being able to provide. In this day and age, everybody works. But if you're not workin', you're not providin'. It's hard to consider a man a man if you ain't bringin' nothin' to the table.

CHRIS: Both my grandfather and my father were in the military. My dad was in Vietnam. My grandfather was in World War II. So they were both stern figures. Discipline. Didn't take no mess. I think I've gotten that from the way we raise our children. Being respectful. Stayin' on task. Disciplinin'. Just being that stern figure. I've gotten that from my father.

My dad, he didn't take too much nonsense. People call me Chris. My name is Christopher. My dad, *to this day,* has *never* called me Chris. He calls me by my government name. So that just goes to show you, havin' that military-type background, that it was serious. You know when your parents call you by your full name, you better come runnin'. I've taken all those things from my dad. Just bein' stern. Bein' there. Bein' that head figure.

TIFFANI: I think a man should be supportive. Definitely hardworking. He should be able to listen. As well as be able to give. He should, at least, show effort of tryin' to make things happen. The major thing is bein' a man of your word. That's really important. And just bein' there. Bein' present. Paying' attention to what's goin' on.

CHRIS: When we were havin' our son, Tiff's pregnancy was crazy. It wasn't planned. When we found out she was pregnant, I was like, "Wow." I wasn't ready. Who's really ready? Unless you're trying, who's ready to be a parent, you know? You get hit. Soon as you find out, you have to prepare yourself.

I was scared. I was anxious and excited. All at the same time. But coming into this relationship, my wife had a daughter from a previous relationship. So I had practice. I've been around kids all my life. My mom has a daycare. Growin' up, I have a twin sister. So I've been around kids. Growin' up with kids, it gives you a little bit of a head start.

But finding out that I was about to have one of my own, it was crazy. 'Cause I know that was *our* responsibility. Like I said, when we first met, Tiff had a daughter [Destiny] from a previous relationship. But at the time we were dating, I knew that she wasn't my full responsibility, at that time. But yeah it was stressful. It was a rough pregnancy. But I was excited too.

CHRIS: I think it was stressful until he was born. And the stress ain't less. 'Cause children are a handful. I think the stress calmed down toward the end of the pregnancy. Toward the end, it did kinda calm down, just a little bit.

TIFFANI: I know that it's very difficult, from my perspective, to teach my son certain things. And certain things I just don't know how to 'cause I don't have that body. Things happen that I just don't know about. So it's very important to have a male, a father in my son's life. He asks me questions all the time. I'm like, "I don't know. I don't have that. I don't know how that works. You're gonna have to ask your daddy." There's things that I just don't know because I don't have that anatomy.

But the other thing is, there's times when little boys especially can be very disobedient. And no matter how much I yell or discipline, sometimes Chris can come in, say something, or do somethin', and it's *shut down*. So that's very important.

TIFFANI: In parenting females, I think the most important thing is to have a good male role model. I feel like girls, especially when we're young, the first male that we love is the male role model that's in our life.

That's where we learn affection, the feelin' of bein' loved. I think it's important to have a good role model—male role model—to teach that for a relationship.

My daughter, she has Chris. And you can tell that she respects him. She loves him. It's very, very important because when she starts choosin' her mate, I know that Chris is gonna play a big role in that choice. If he was a bad guy, then I know that there would be a bad guy in my future.

CHRIS: As men, we don't have women parts. Women go through *a lot*. Girls, in their adolescence, they go through a lot. A lot of emotions. A lot of body changing. So I think just being supportive and understanding. Just being available for them to talk to you is always key.

Of course, a lot of times you're gonna have to defer, like, "You need to talk to your mom about that 'cause I don't know anything about that." But just being receptive to things that go on. 'Cause things that go on in the girl's life, young lady's life are way different than things that go on in a young man's life. So being receptive and being open. Being open to have those conversations about Mother Nature.

With boys, being stern, aggressive and being honest with him. Of course, showing love. Always showin' love. Not bein' afraid to say, "I love you, son." 'Cause some dads don't say that to their kids. Especially to their sons. "We love you." Every day, every night. You know, "Love you. Good night. Go to sleep." In the morning, before school, "Love you. Have a good day." I think those things, sayin' you love him, being stern, bein' that no-nonsense type of dad. But at the same time still bein' able to play with my child. You got to have balance. It's hard to balance, but it's something that you *have to do*.

TIFFANI: It's important to have that balance. For our son to know that you can't hold onto things. That's actually a life lesson. You get in trouble. Things happen. But you can't wallow in it. You have to keep movin'. It's important to be able to switch and move forward. I do believe in disciplining my kids physically. That's how I was raised.

As far as our kids, we don't have to physically discipline them very often. Growin' up, I got physically disciplined *often*. My mom does not play. But with our kids there's so many electronic things you can take away from them. We get a better response when we say, "You can't play Skylanders," or "Give me your cell phone." That hurts them more than us physically doin' somethin' to them. Getting a whoopin' is short-term. Spur of the moment. That goes away.

CHRIS: There's a gray line with the discipline. You don't want your child to think that if you're mad at somebody you have to fight 'em. Or you gotta beat 'em. So you gotta know when a whoopin' is necessary and when a punishment might be necessary. Not a beatin'. Nobody goin' to jail. No blood.

CHRIS: Prior to Tiff and I dating, I was dating another woman who had a child. So it wasn't new. But it was still *different*. 'Cause, of course, all children are different. So I think the major thing when you're dating someone with a child is you have to able to know that the child is gonna come first. You can't always call and be like, "Can we go to the movies? Can we go out to dinner?" That lady—that woman—has a child.

If the child doesn't have somewhere to go, a babysitter, a dad's house to go to, you're not goin' out. So you have to be able to understand that you're not gonna come first at all times. Especially when you're dating. 'Cause you're not the number-one priority. That child is *always* number one. You will fall to the bottom of that list real quick. And you gotta understand that. It's hard for some people to understand.

But I knew that coming into our relationship Tiff was a great mother. She was always there for her child. So for me, that was the first thing I noticed about dating a woman that already had a child. That time, you may not get it all the time. But when you get it, it's valuable.

Of course, there were times when I was irritated or upset. I don't know if it was just me bein' immature or what. So I just rolled with it. And it's because I wanted to get to know her. If you're in that situation and you're not interested in that woman, you will probably go, "Okay, whatever. I don't have time for that." But I was *extremely* interested. You see the wedding ring. So it paid off!

TIFFANI: Our situation was a little different from just us dating and meeting out of the blue. We were actually good friends for about two years first. So my daughter already knew Chris because we worked together at a different hair shop. My daughter knew everybody I worked with. So she already knew, "Chris is fun. He colors with me." Because we were friends.

Chris had already come over the house. So she was already comfortable with him. I was kinda past that point. Before Chris, out of the people I dated, only one person had met my daughter. I didn't want her to have that in and out, in and out, this guy, that guy thing. My thing was that a guy had to be sane, of course. I had to make sure that they were safe around children in general. Make sure that they weren't just strange, didn't feel strange. I would have liked them to have been around kids that I know. Or just see them interact with some children first. If they just feel *wrong,* I'm done. Like a woman's intuition.

I dated people and I just didn't feel like they were worthy of meeting my child. I didn't want them around her. I didn't want her to say, "What happened to this guy?" when he ended up disappearing. So I made a very strong effort to keep them on *their* side and keep my daughter on *her* side. I didn't even tell them my child's name unless it was a year or year and a half down the road.

A man would definitely have to demonstrate some patience. That's very important. When you introduce somebody new to your child, they usually test 'em. They usually do somethin' horrible. They act up because they wanna see what they're gonna do. Kids know what's goin' on. Don't underestimate a child because children are very smart.

It's just so many things you have to look out for. You have to protect your kids. Pay attention to the person. The way they talk. You might not want your kids around somebody that's cursin' all the time 'cause you don't want them to repeat it. You want someone to dress appropriately. Talk, dress, and smell appropriate. As a woman, you should be lookin' for someone that you think you would *want* to present to your children, you know? You shouldn't be datin' somebody that you wouldn't want to be around your kids. Somebody that you wouldn't want to have kids with.

CHRIS: With Destiny, bein' that she's a girl, I had to approach things totally differently. I had to be sensitive to her feelings. Firstly, "There's a man living with me that's not my dad." Who knows how a young girl's mind is thinking' about that?

So I kinda walked a fine line. To this day, I've *never* whooped Destiny. I don't feel comfortable. I didn't feel comfortable disciplining her physically because that's not my biological child. Plus, her dad, he's around. He's present.

When we first started dating, my mom asked me, "Are you gonna have Destiny call you dad?" I was like, "No." If her dad was gone, that would be somethin' to discuss. At that time, Destiny and her father had a good relationship. So I didn't want her to feel like she *had to* call me dad. She can just call me Chris. If she ever feels to the point where she *wants to* call me dad, then I'm gonna accept it. But I never wanted to force the issue. That could be uncomfortable.

So goin' into our marriage and relationship, I wanted to be sensitive to Destiny's feelings. She's fifteen years old now. It's a lotta emotion. A lotta attitude. It's crazy now. But it's a gratifying feeling. We have friends that tell us all the time, "Man, you're such a good dad. You've done such a good thing with bein' in Destiny's life, man. I know a lotta men that wouldn't put themselves in that position."

Destiny doesn't say it, but I know she respects and she appreciates the things that I do for her. It's just something that I feel. So with me going into being a father to another man's child—*a girl at that*—the key thing was bein' sensitive to the situation.

Yeah, we have butted heads a couple times. And she's told me, "You're not my dad! I wanna go stay with my dad!" I've been through that. And that hurts. That really hurts when you've been there for so long. When you've supported them and been there.

TIFFANI: Of course, they're gonna say that. Every child says that. Even if Chris wasn't around, she would have said that to me, I'm sure. It happens.

CHRIS: It's a constant battle, though. Raisin' children, period, is a constant battle. You're not always gonna agree. You're gonna have your ups and downs. Just try your best to lead them in the right way. And try your best not to get too steamed when it's a tough situation. You gotta keep a cool head. *Especially* in the situation where you're not the biological father.

Things could get twisted and turned if somethin' were to ever happen bad. Destiny could go tell her dad, and that would be a whole 'nother issue. So you have to think about a lotta that stuff when you're in a relationship raisin' someone else's child.

With her biological father, we've had our ups and downs. We've been cool, and we've not been cool. Our interaction now is we're cordial. We see each other, it's respect. When Tiff and I were datin', it was another story. We were clashin'. You know, when you have a daughter and another guy is in the picture, it takes a lot to be able to watch somebody take *your* place.

But we've hung out. I don't think a lotta people can say that. We've had a pretty good relationship through the years. Some things, of course, we would change. Some things we'd take back. But honestly, it's okay. It hasn't been terrible ride.

TIFFANI: I let Chris do Chris. There's only so much he's gonna do. Only so far he's gonna go. I do encourage our daughter to be respectful. Sometimes she can teeter on that line of disrespect and respect because she's a teenager. She's feelin' herself.

As far as the bridge between the two men, her biological father is the total opposite of Chris. He doesn't have that good foundation, that good father and grandfather foundation. So he works on feelings. His discipline is based off of how he feels and how he believes Destiny feels. He feels like she's his duplicate, basically. Which is not true, but in some aspects, is true. It's difficult to come to a common ground with him, as far as discipline. So I just let him say what he wants to say. I listen, respectfully. And I tell him my view.

CHRIS: Destiny calls me Chris. And my son, Christopher, has never thought about callin' me Chris. He's always called me dad. When he was small, it was funny because he was tryin' to grasp it. Like, "Daddy's *not* your dad?" He still tries to figure it out, but he's eight now. He knows who her biological father is. But it's funny because he was really tryin' to wrap his brain around the fact that, "Mommy, that's mommy. But Daddy, that's *not your* daddy. You don't call Daddy dad. You don't call him daddy." So he's asked a few questions, but that hasn't been too much of an issue.

TIFFANI: I don't think so either. The only time it becomes an issue with me is when *this* child goes to *this* grandparent and *that* child goes to *that* grandparent. I wish they could go to the same grandparent. But fortunately, my daughter is the only child in her family. And Christopher is an only child in my other family. So they both equally get spoiled, so it's great! It balances out perfect. I don't feel like one is getting more than the other. They get too much *equally*.

TIFFANI: I do think men need to play a bigger role. I do see a lotta women that are single parents. And although they are doin' it and makin' it work, payin' their bills, bein' mom and dad, they don't enjoy it. They're doin' it because they *have* to. They're not doin' it because that's what they chose to do, most of them.

As a stylist, I get to hear this all the time. And they would love to have a male that could step up to the plate, or the dad that was there. Even if they're not together with the dad, they would love for him to be present. There's a lotta women that are single moms, and the dads don't do *anything*.

I hear stories of them not payin' child support. Women takin' them to court. Just a lotta negative things. And the women are *exhausted*. It's really difficult to be a mom *and* a dad. It's impossible. I think a lotta men need to look in the mirror. They're too busy lookin' at, "Well, I was with her, and we had this kid together, and *now* she wants this and that." It's really not about that. It's about the child. The child is the most important part of the relationship.

Even if you don't wanna be with that woman, you need to help this child. And I see that so often. It's really sad because the child is the person that really is not getting what they need to become a good adult. That cycle might continue because of that. That seed has been planted.

But there *are* good fathers, like Chris. He has a lotta clients that are good fathers, even step-parents. They're just doin' what they're *supposed* to do. I see them come in the shop with their sons or daughters, their babies. And they don't miss a beat.

So I think it's really, really important. We need to see that more. It needs to happen more. It's a stereotype in our Black community that you're gonna have a baby, he might be there with you, he might not. He might keep movin' on to have more babies with other people. It's very rare in our community for a man to have a baby and stay with the baby and the mom. And get married too. I think it's important to have that in our community. It needs to be increased, definitely.

CHRIS: I think it's a trying time right now. There's a lot of kids out there missin' their fathers. It's very sad the way we see our future, the children. That's *our future*. And seein' what they're doin' and what they're gettin'

themselves into right now, it's rough. And a lot of that is because they haven't had a father or father figure. They don't have somebody to look up to. Or the guys they're lookin' up to are the same guys that are on the corner. That's their role models. So it's very important to have someone in a child's life.

Kids out there, they don't have a good role model. Or they don't have the *right* role model, men to look up to. It's important that children see their parents interacting positively because that plays a major role in how they'll be in a relationship.

As far as in today's world you see a lot of Black men not bein' there for their kids. But the problem is there's so many that are. But the number that *aren't* just outshine those that *are.* So we just get a bad rap. And nobody's perfect. We all fall short. But make that effort to be in your child's life. Try and do things positively. You have to be physically present and do things with your children. There's a lotta small things that you can do. It's all about bein' positive. We just gotta do better.

TIFFANI: I think it's something that needs to be addressed. I haven't seen *anything* on Black fathers, positive Black fathers. It's always, "They're missing. Where are they?" But to put them, to showcase them, I think is great. It needs to be done. It's definitely a blank space.

CHRIS: It's necessary. This is a story that *needs* to be told. Just hearing it from the fathers. Comin' outta their mouth—their opinions, their situations—is important. Once you hear it from them, it's solidified. It's their truth. Their opinion. It's how they feel about the situation. I know a couple people who are in crazy situations, have a couple of kids, but who are great fathers. I'm glad. It just needs to be told. Our light needs to be shined brighter, as Black fathers. I just hope more Black fathers put more effort into being good fathers.

Being a dad is not the same as being a father. You can be a dad and have twelve kids and never seen not one of 'em. That doesn't make you a *father*. Bein' a father is being there. Being supportive. Being able to talk to your children to relate to your children.

TIFFANI: I am proud that I have Chris, for one. He does it effortlessly. He definitely knows what he's doin'. He's doin a great job. I think it's good that he's a part of both of our kids' life. He could have chosen to not be with me after he found out I was pregnant. I could have been left with another child. Another fatherless child, basically. But he stepped to the plate, and he's still here. He helps me with everything. He gives me a different perspective on things.

With Chris, together, we're able to give our kids more. I thank God for Chris. I feel like we are where we are supposed to be. And I'm so happy that it's him and not my ex. He's a great father. A great dad from the beginning. He definitely is a great part of our lives. He listens to me when I tell him how I feel. And he respects it. We're able to bounce off of each other to make him a great dad. And he makes me, in turn, a great mom. A great mother.

Postscript by Dr. Khalid Akil White

I TRULY APPRECIATE YOUR TIME in reading *Black Fatherhood: Trials & Tribulations, Testimony & Triumph.* Hopefully, you end this book with a renewed energy, renewed purpose and newfound appreciation of Black fathers; our experiences, as well as our commitment. Please keep in mind that the men in this book and, by extension, Black fathers everywhere, are currently helping to raise the next generation of fathers, mothers and future leaders.

Again, this book is intended to challenge the predominant stereotype that Black fathers are absent. Regardless of the situations and circumstances faced, the men in this project have shown the world that it is possible and it is *essential* to remain an active, present father. No matter what, we can do it. And as exhibited in this book, you can see that we've *been* doing it. The role, work and responsibilities of a father are not easy. However, the rewards are great!

As a community, let's continue to build up our families, strengthen each other and actively support our women. Finally, as men, let's reclaim our rightful position as fathers, father figures, mentors, role models and leaders. PEACE.

Afterword by Thurman V. White, Jr.

But the Lord God called to the man, Where are you?

GENESIS 3:9

Where are you?

I AM HONORED TO WRITE this note. For my son, Dr. Khalid Akil White, to invite me, his father, to write an afterword on his project about Black fatherhood makes me "Hallelujah" happy! I must give God all thanks for this Divine assignment. First, thanks that Akil has seen the need to tackle this vital subject. Next, thanks that he thinks enough of our father-son experiences over the years to ask me to say a word about a subject dear to both of us, and a role that he knows I try earnestly to live out to my best. My prayer is this project will provide hope, help, and healing for African American (and all) fathers who seek to be the fathers that God is calling us to become.

"Where are you?" is an age-old question that both comforts and challenges men. If we know God, then being in His presence should give us comfort and confidence. But if we don't know God or we're hiding from Him because of our disobedience, then this question challenges and convicts us. God first asked Adam the question in the Garden of Eden. But this question remains relevant for African American men today. Where are we in leading and loving our families and in building better communities for them? Where are we in taking the time to learn how to become better fathers? Where are we in being transparent and sharing with other fathers—and even our children, wives, and others—our hopes, fears, and even our failures as fathers so we can learn from each other and become better at this essential societal role? "Where are you?" then questions our commitment and calls us to action.

The life experiences and images portrayed in this project inspire and inform us. They depict men as real fathers—not perfect by any means (and

I would be the first to admit that my fathering has not always been what I'd hoped it could be consistently). But these images and interviews show men who are hopeful and striving to participate actively in the most important role any man can play: to nurture your children to become mature adults who in turn can become productive fathers and mothers in their generation. Most of all, we see many diverse and encouraging models of Black male love for our children, families, and communities.

It's ironic that the most important life roles we've been asked to play—as husbands and fathers—don't come with any instruction manual other than the Bible and the conflicting good and bad habits we observe from our own parents and the world's culture. Most of what we've learned on our own through the generations we should unlearn. We can't have a better playbook than God's word, the fellowship of other men, and the power of prayer and the Holy Spirit to help us to positively change our trajectory as Black fathers.

I believe this book and the video will become resources that can be passed among men and within families to stimulate dialogue and learning. Perhaps Khalid's next book can be on Black fathers and grandfathers! And maybe I can collaborate with him. We often miss opportunities for intergenerational learning because men of all ages don't honestly discuss their life experiences with each other. Hopefully, *Black Fatherhood* will motivate us to do more sharing and caring.

Thurman V. White, Jr. (Dad and Grandpa)
San Francisco, California

About the Author

KHALID AKIL WHITE IS A professor of African American studies at San Jose City College and San Jose State University. He has a bachelor of arts from Morehouse College, a master of education from Harvard University Graduate School of Education, and a doctorate in education from UC Davis and Sonoma State University.

Khalid White lives in the San Francisco Bay Area with his wife and daughter.

He is a co-author of *Teaching Men of Color in Community College Guidebook* (2015) and a contributing author to the *Street Lit Anthology* (2014).

White won the 2015 Man of the Year Award from the Striving Black Brothers Coalition (SBBC) at Chabot College and the 2011 Outstanding Male Faculty Award, from San Jose City College.

He is a recognized mentor with Silicon Valley's Oriki Theater Rites of Passage Program (2015-16).

Khalid's hobbies include reading, writing, travel, cooking, entrepreneurship and sports.

If you support this book, please support Khalid's feature-length documentary film, also entitled: *Black Fatherhood: Trials & Tribulations, Testimony & Triumph.* Use the hyper link for more details:
https://youtu.be/R5-pvROhdDo

You can connect with Khalid through his website www.blkmpwr.com
Or, via social media, on Instagram @blkmpwr and Twitter @brother_white.

Works Cited

"Be" (Intro) by Common. 2005

"6 Actual Facts Shatter the Biggest Stereotypes of Black Fathers" by Antwuan Sargent. www.mic.com June 14, 2014.

"Black Co-Parenting" by Krystal Glass. May 2013.

"Don't Call them Mr. Mom" by Brigid Schulte. www.washingtonpost.com Statistics by Pew Research Center. June 5, 2014.

"Family Reunion" by the O'Jays. 1975

The Holy Bible

Luhya Proverb from www.afritorial.com

Merriam-Webster's Online Dictionary 2009.

"The Myth of the Absent Black Father" by Tara Culp-Ressler. www.thinkprogress.org January 16, 2014.

The Steve Harvey Morning Show

Dr. W.E.B. DuBois